LET'S COLOR
A SUPERHERO STORY

AN INCLUSIVE COLORING BOOK FOR MINDFULNESS AND RESILIENCE

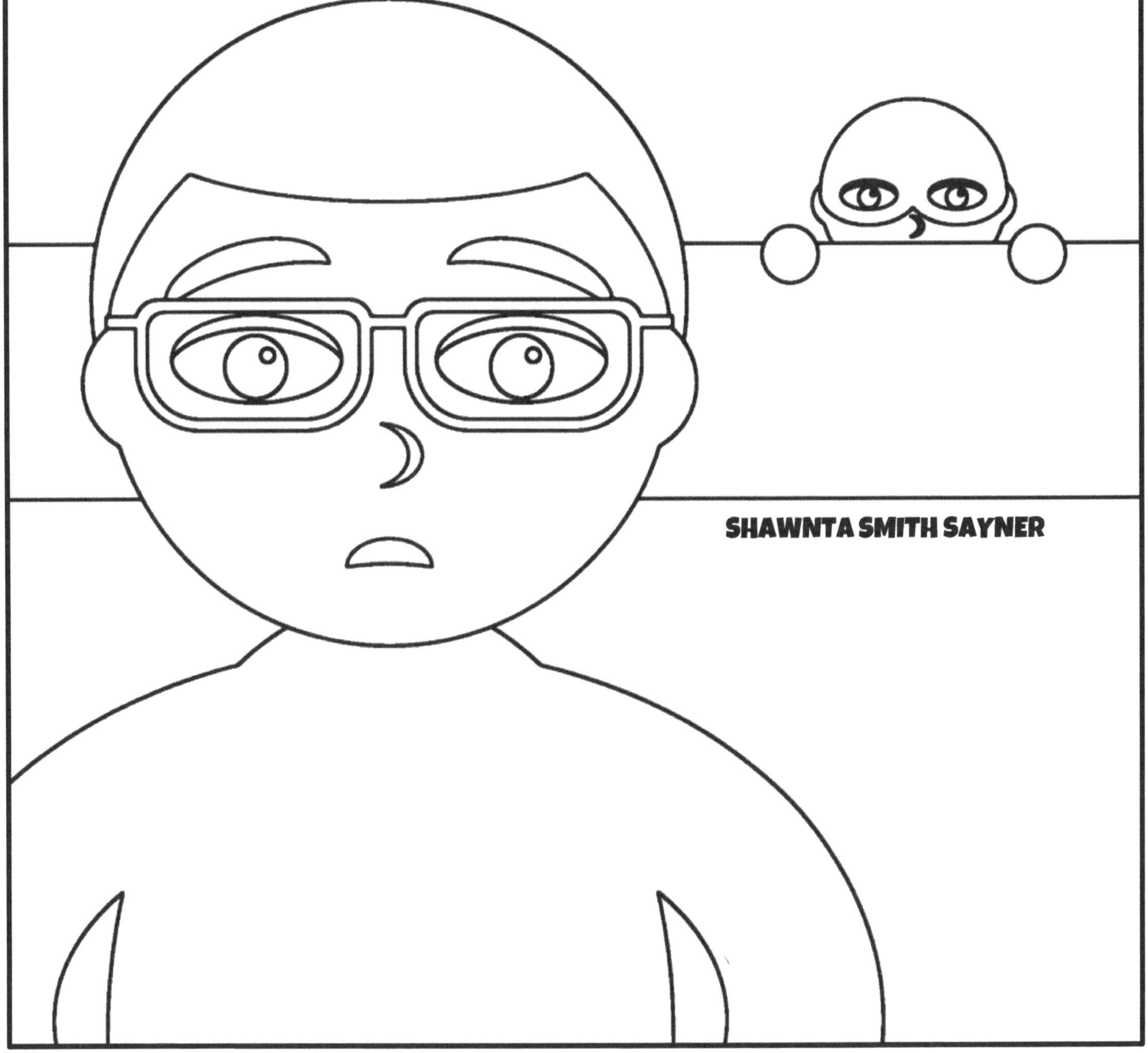

SHAWNTA SMITH SAYNER

Library of Congress Cataloging-in-Publication Data available
Library of Congress Control Number: 2021909098
ISBN: 978-1-952944-13-0

First Edition: May 2021

THIS BOOK BELONGS TO

I CAN BE BRAVE

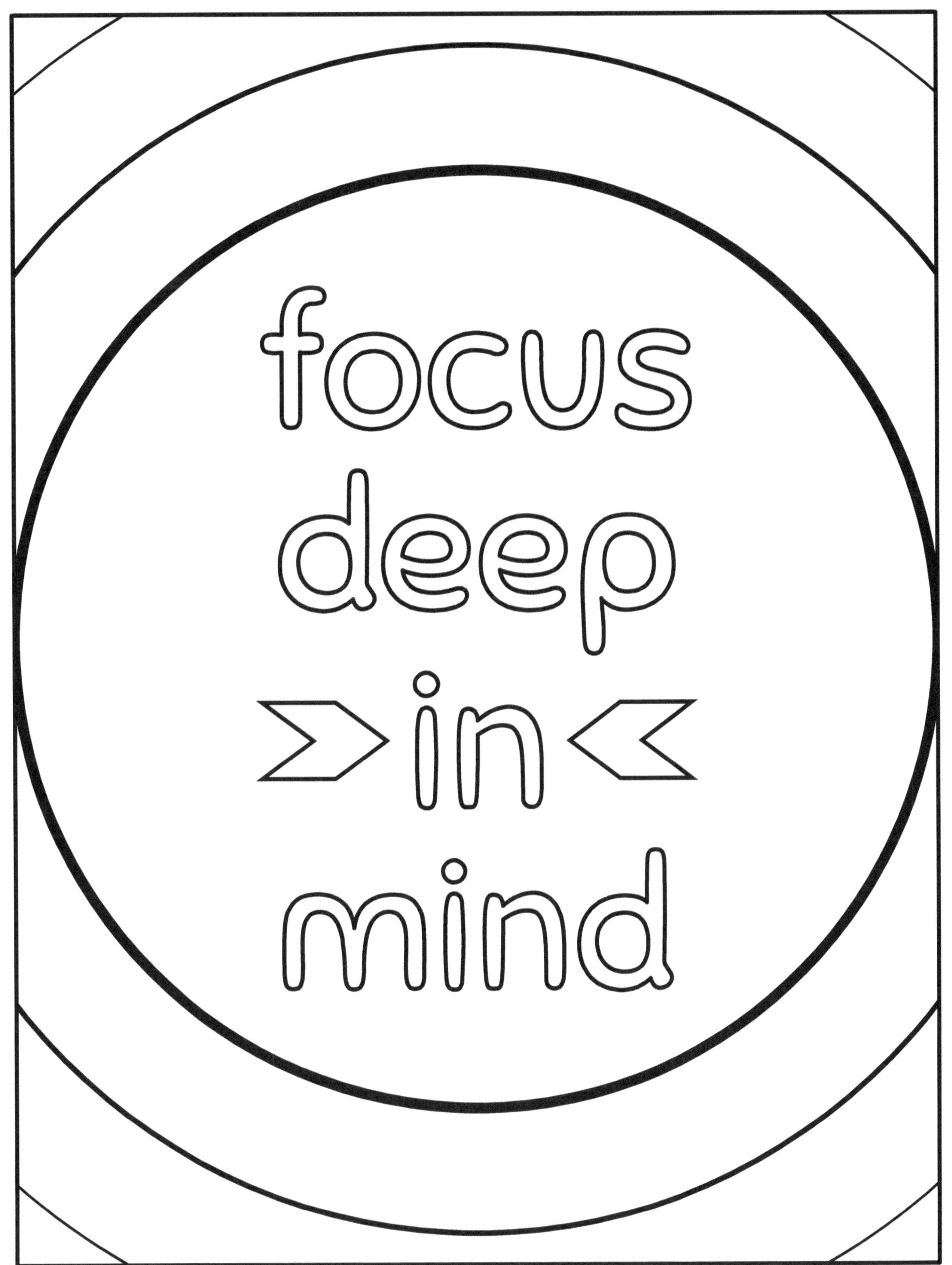

focus
deep
>in<
mind

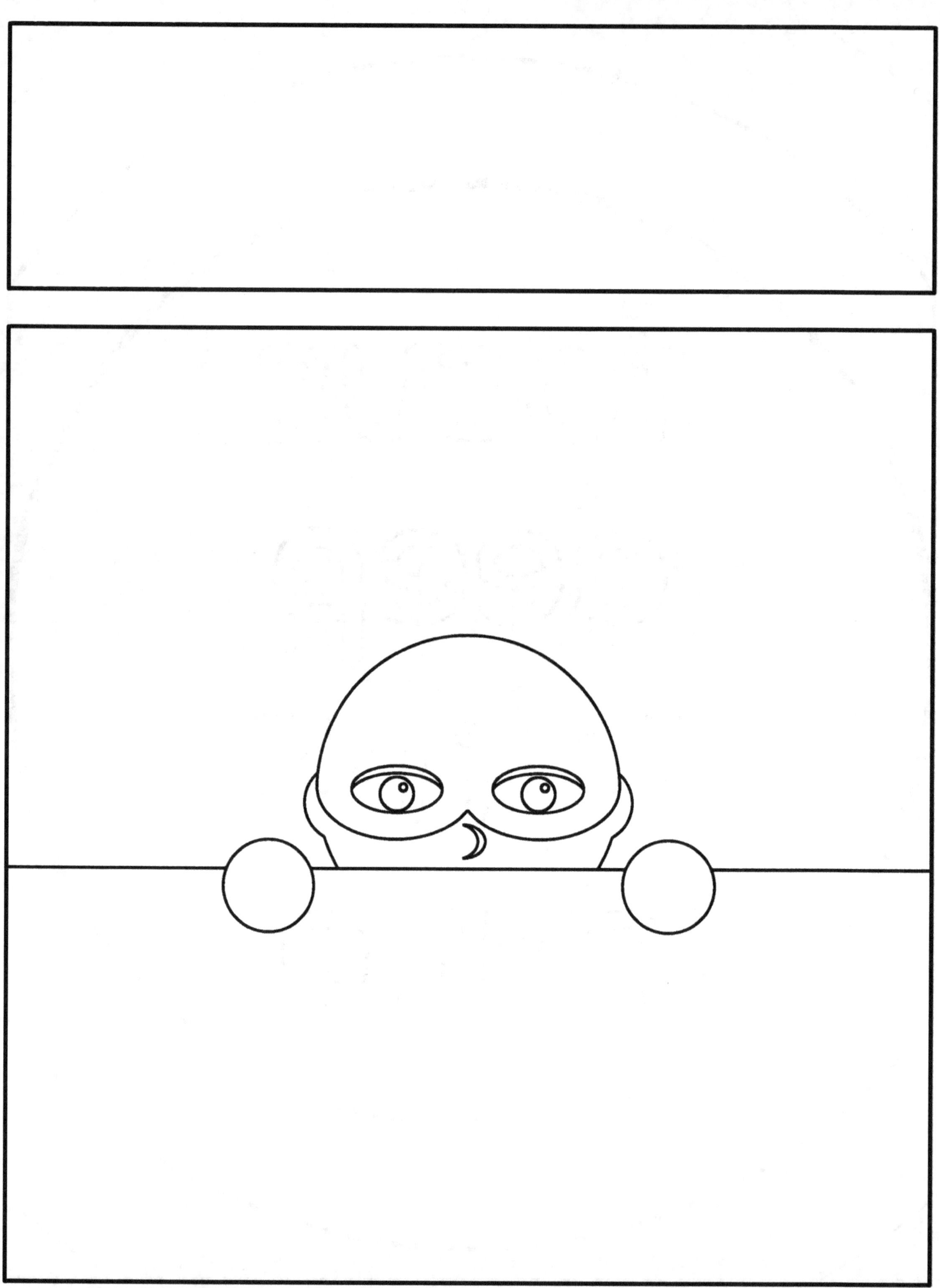

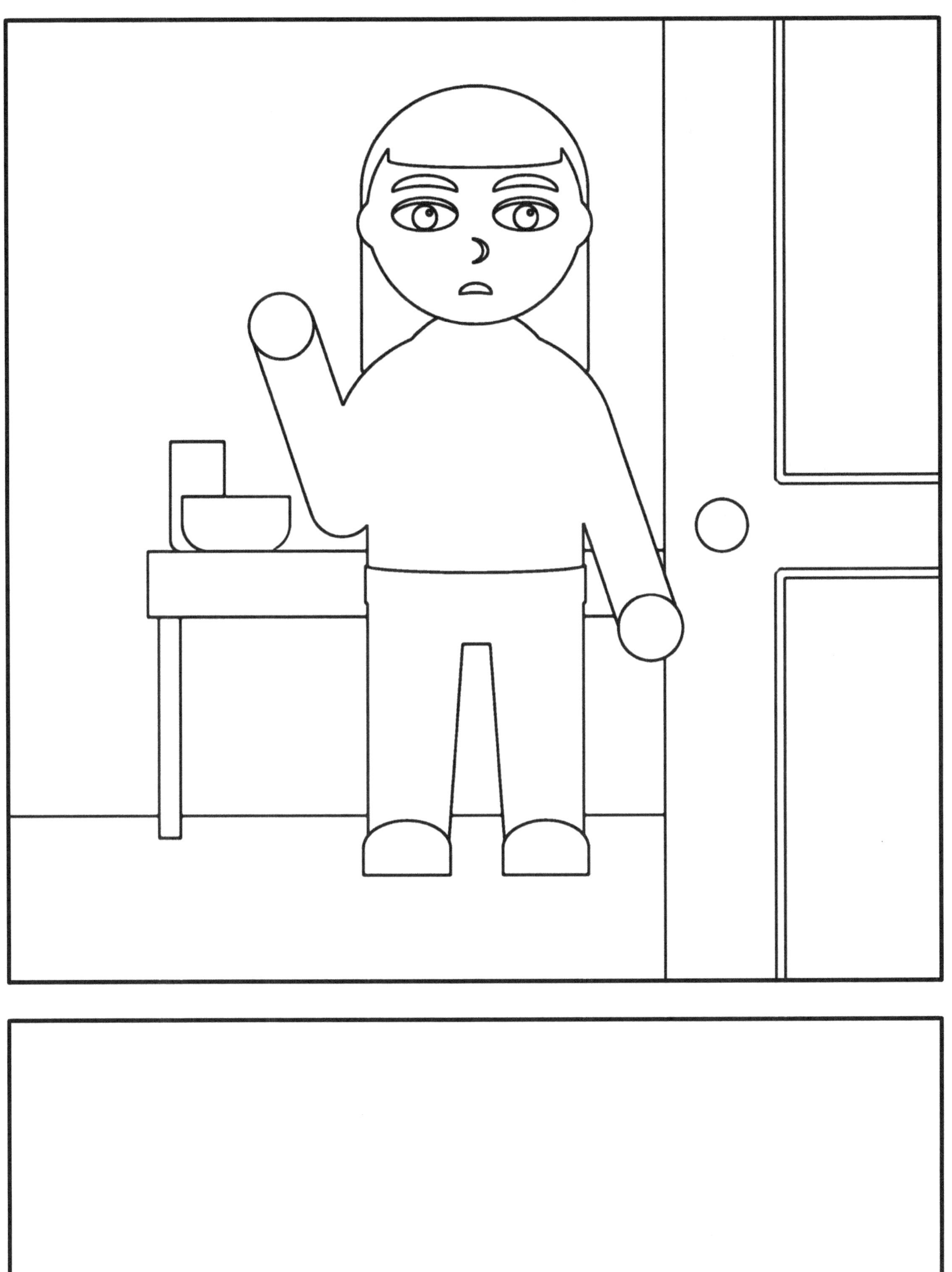

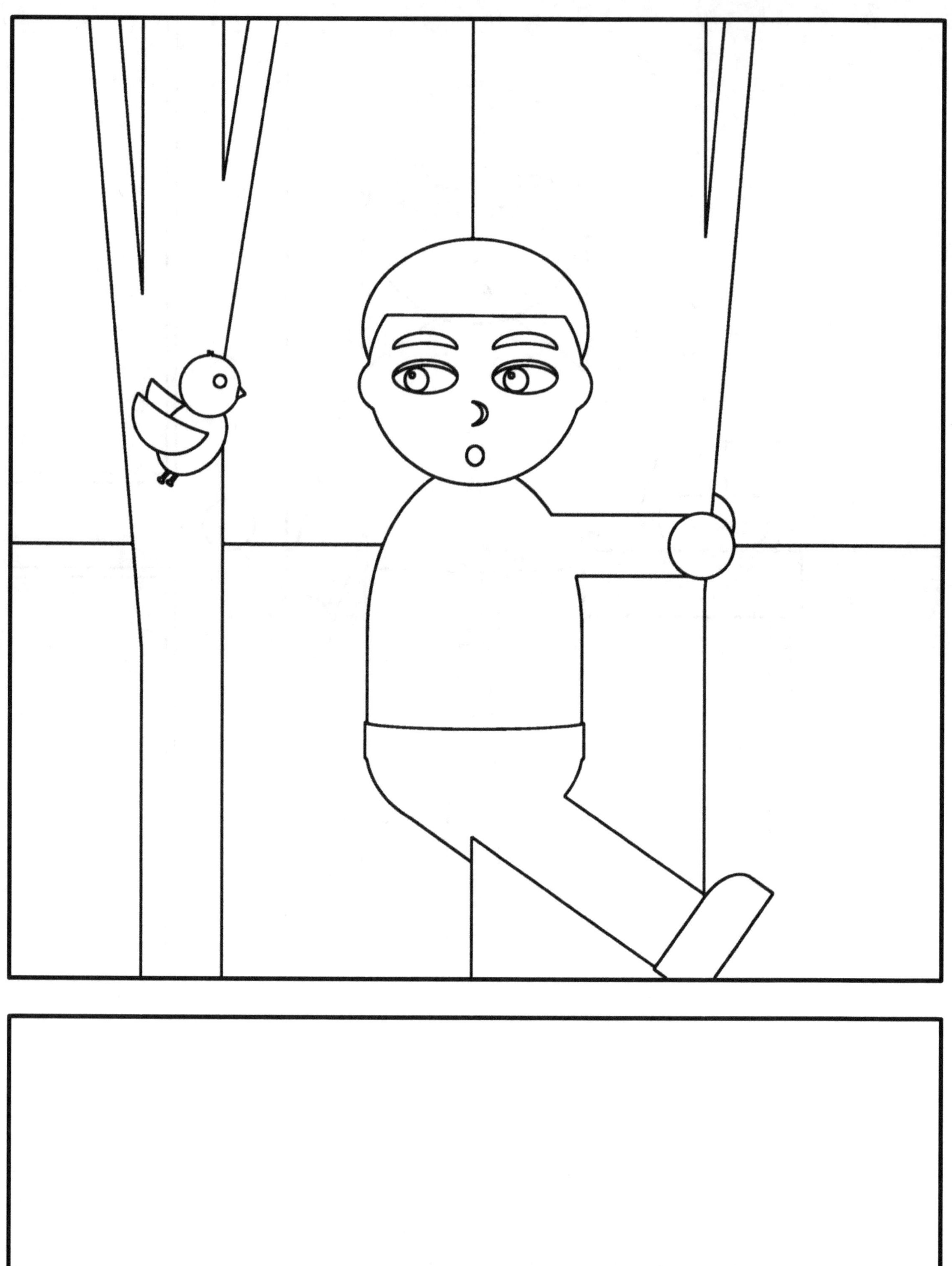

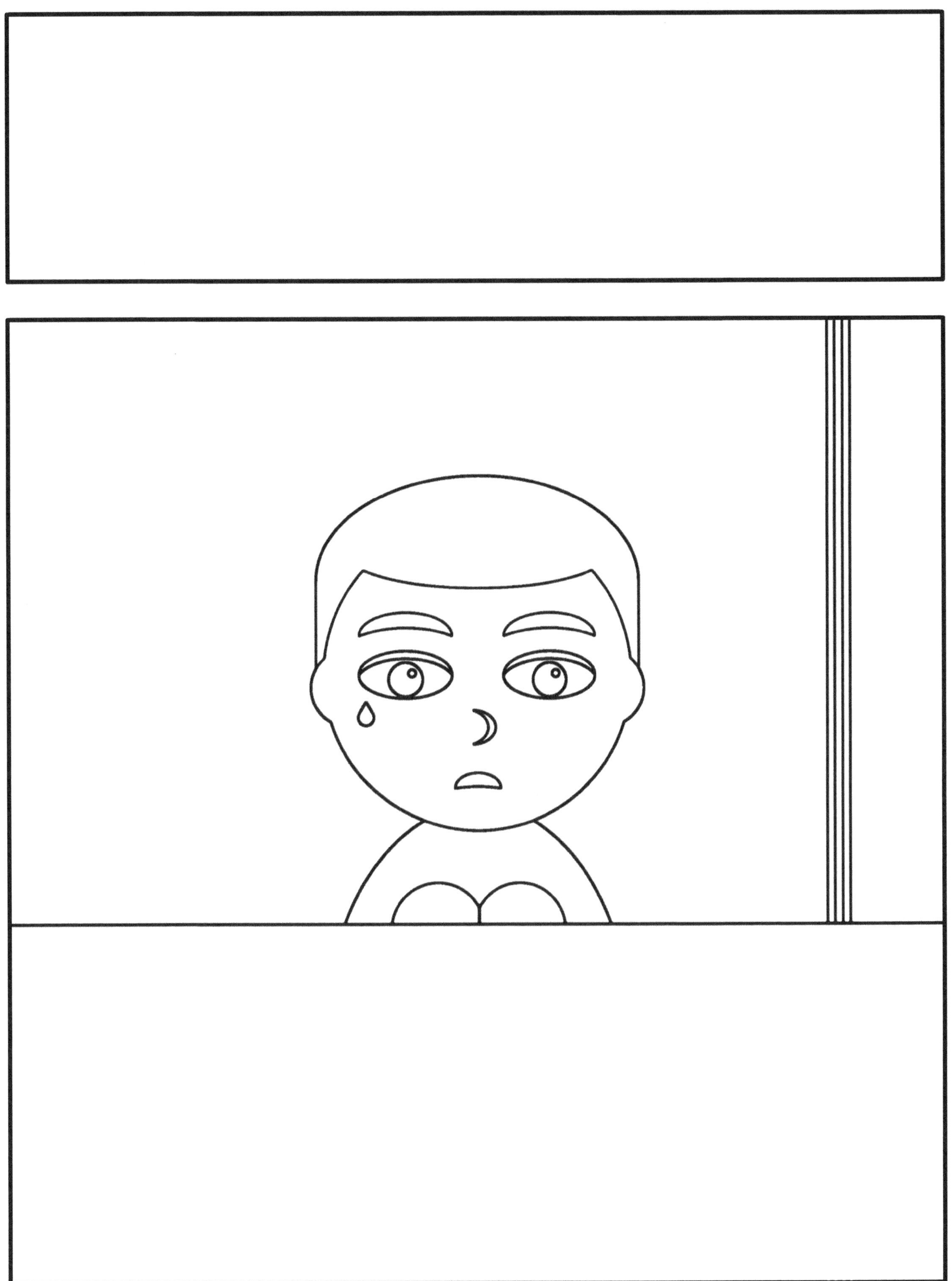

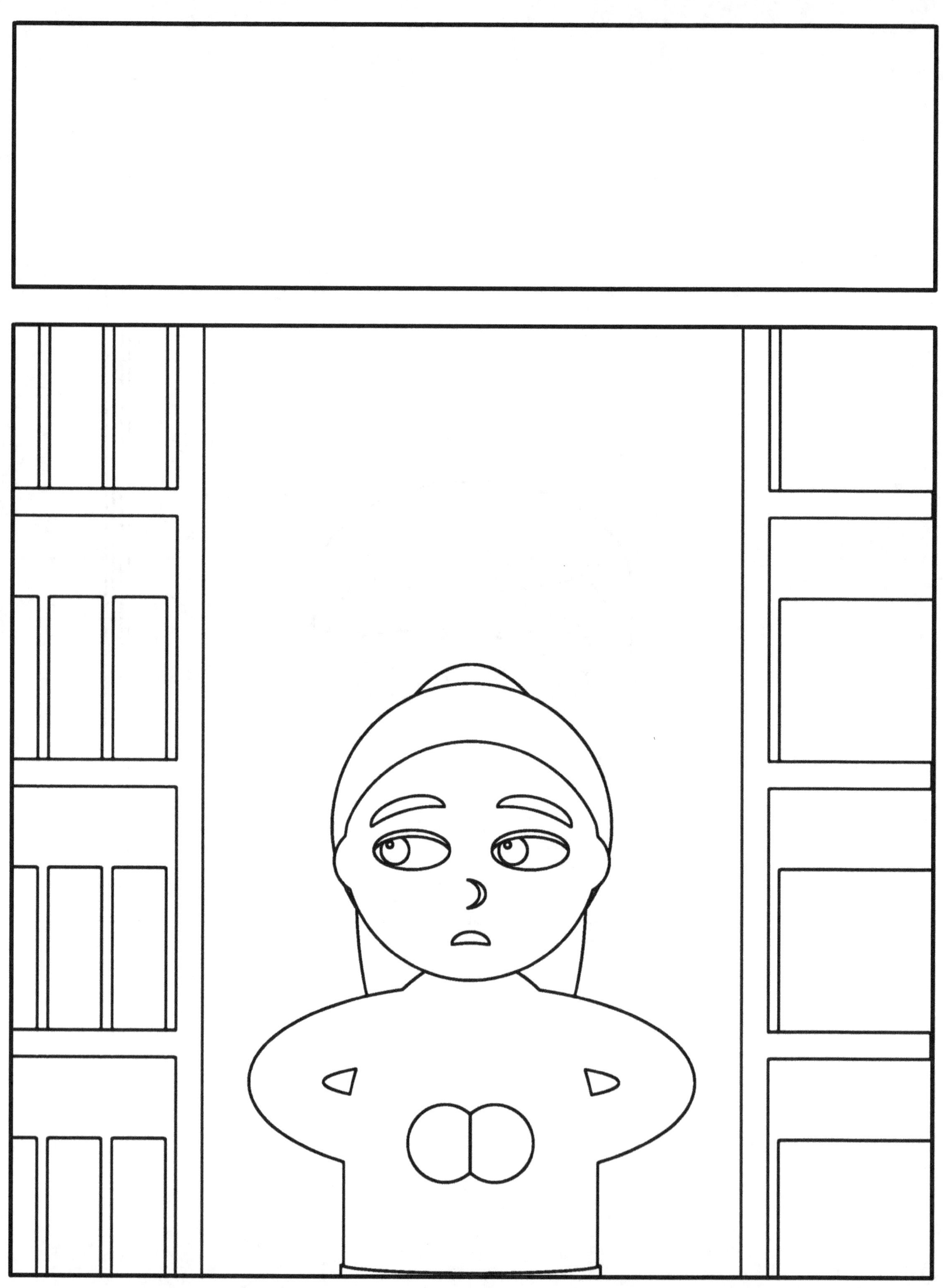

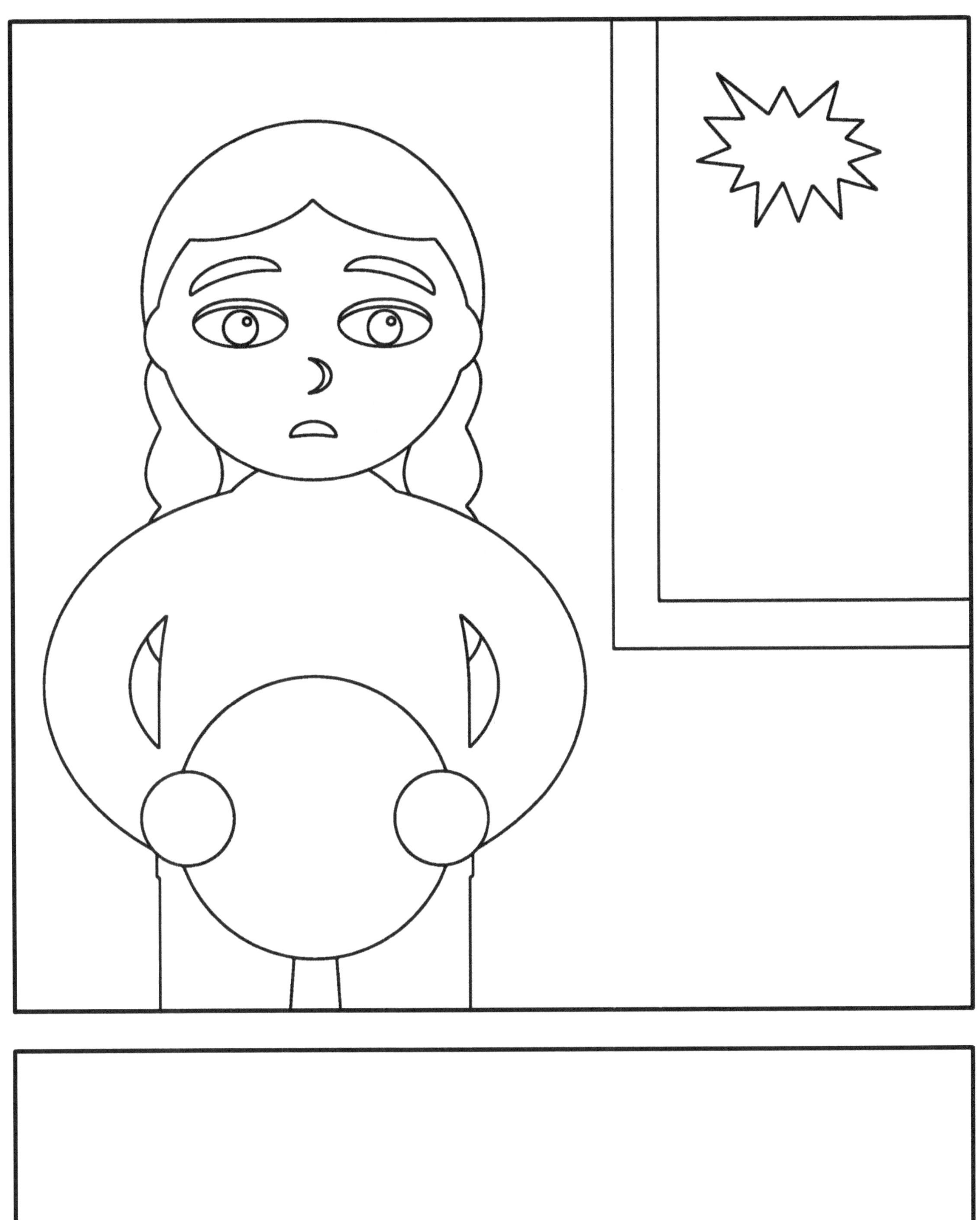

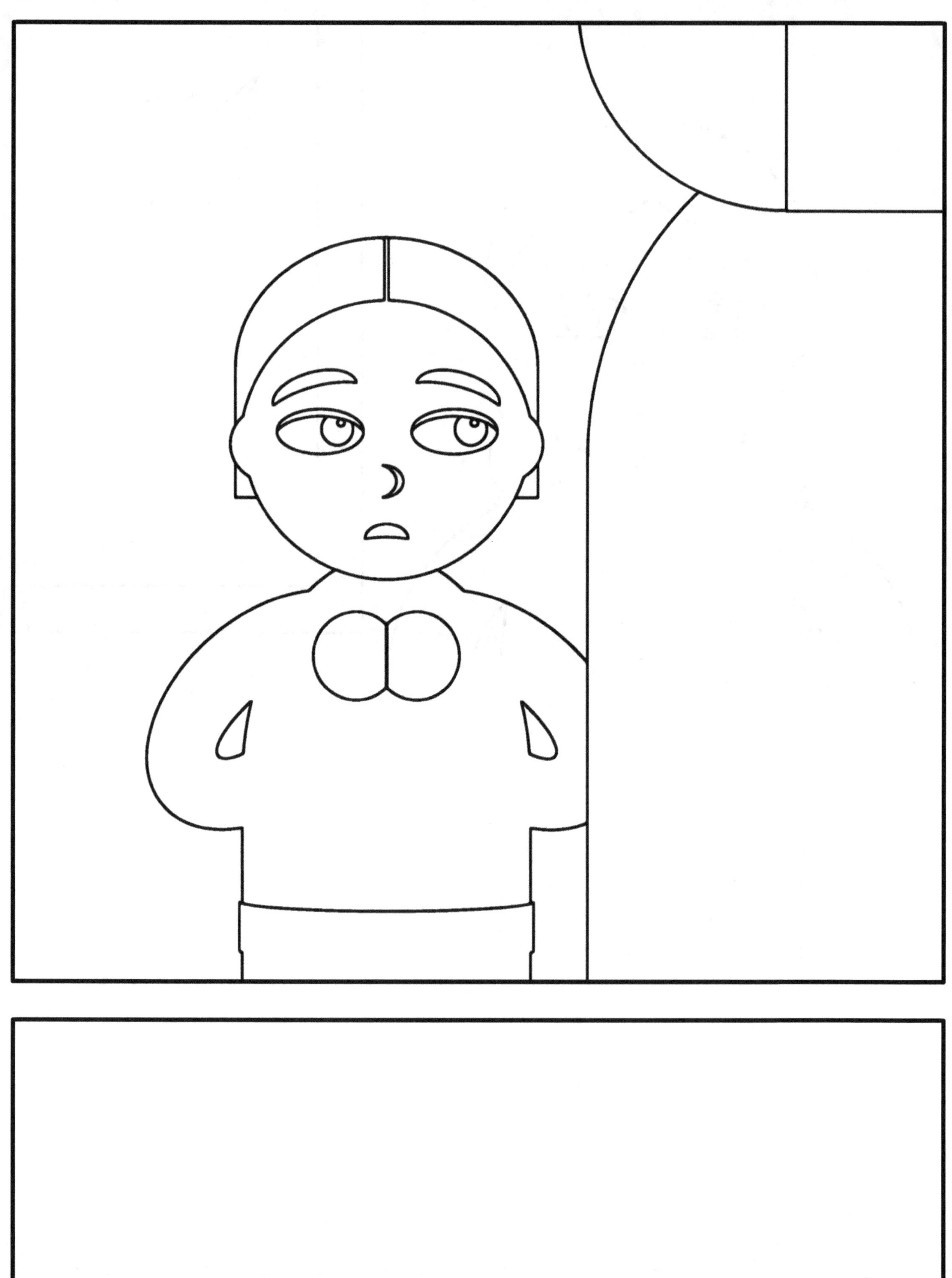

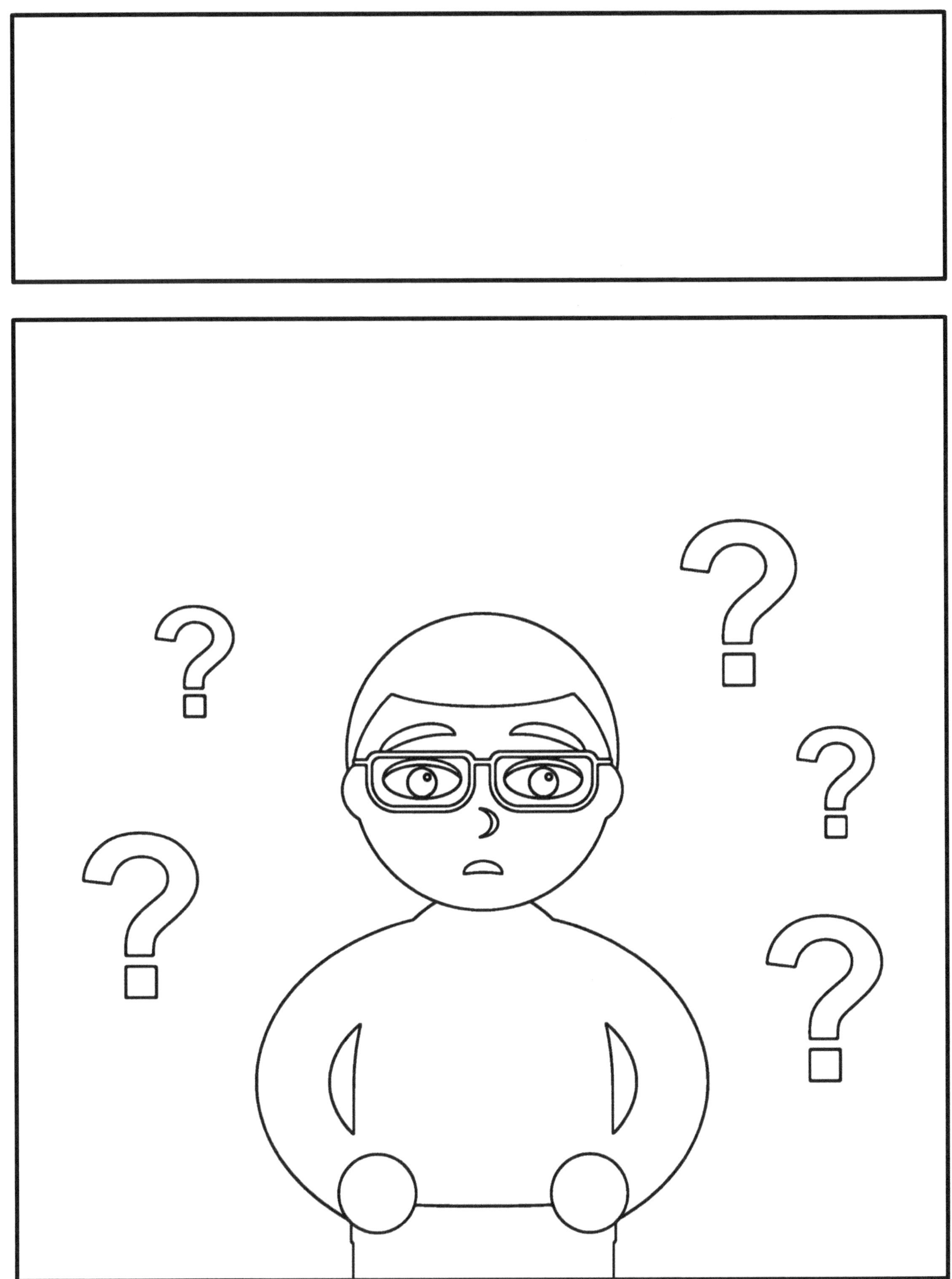

I CAN DO HARD THINGS

I am

stronger

than

rough tough

stuff

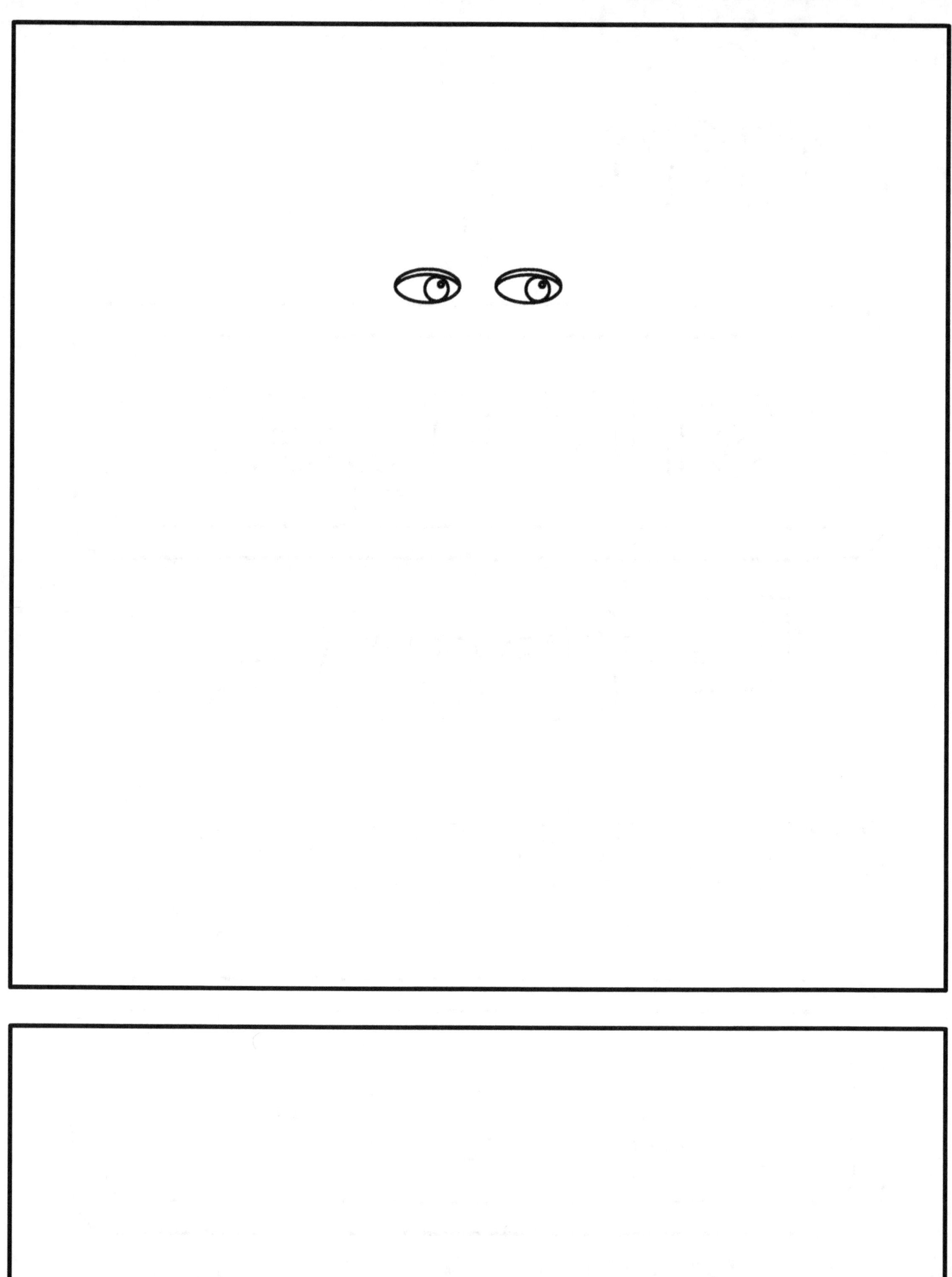

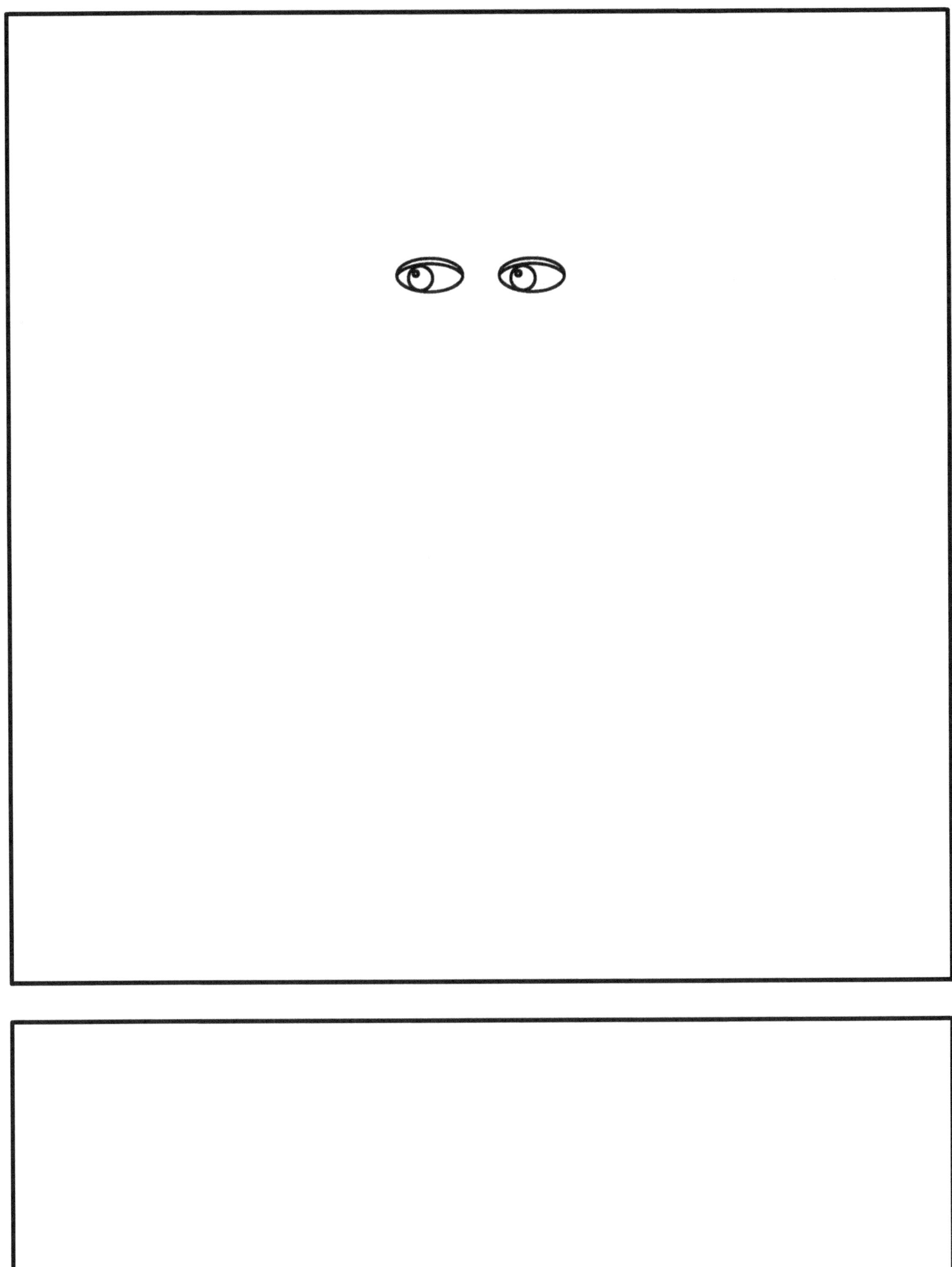

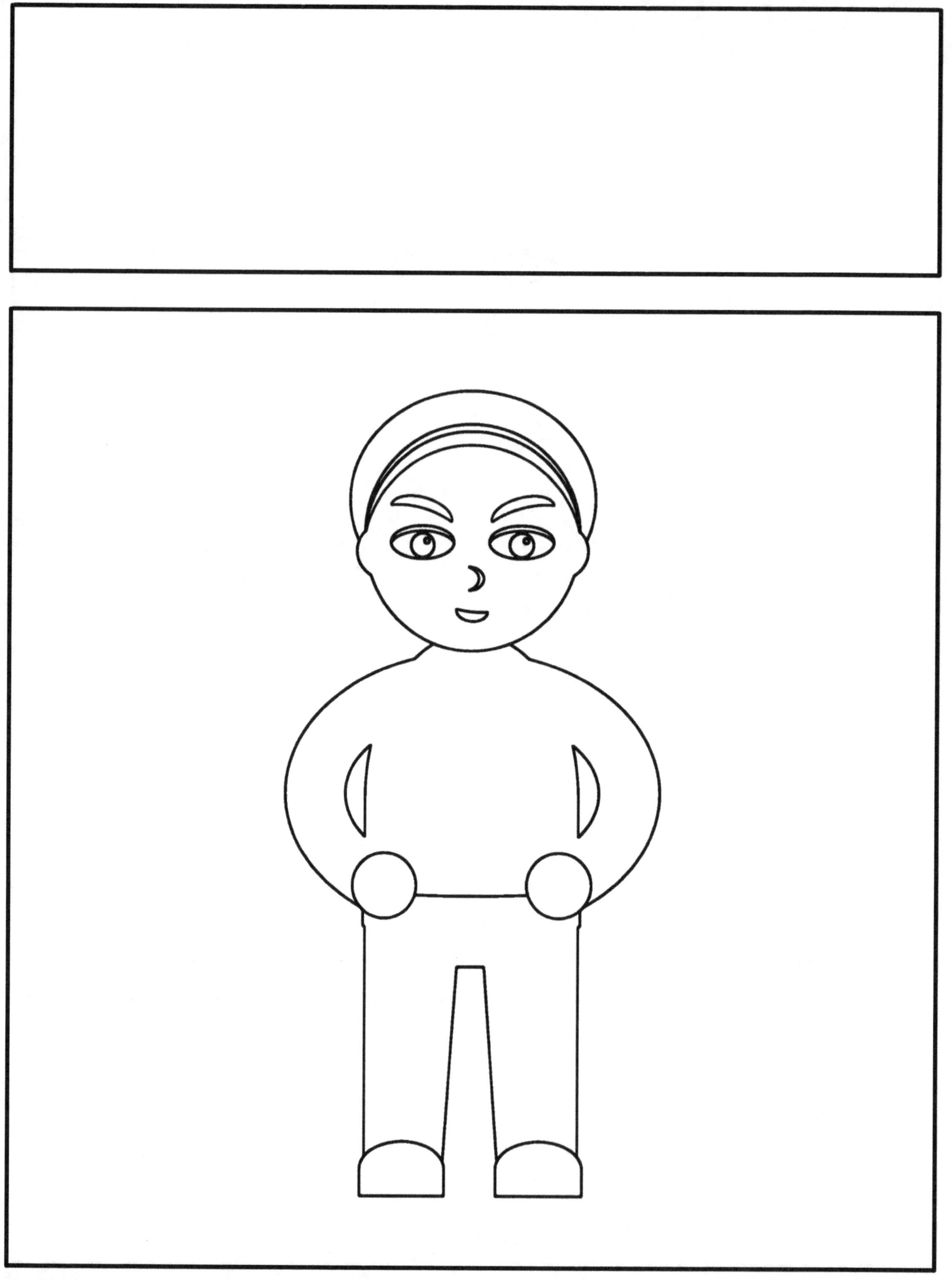

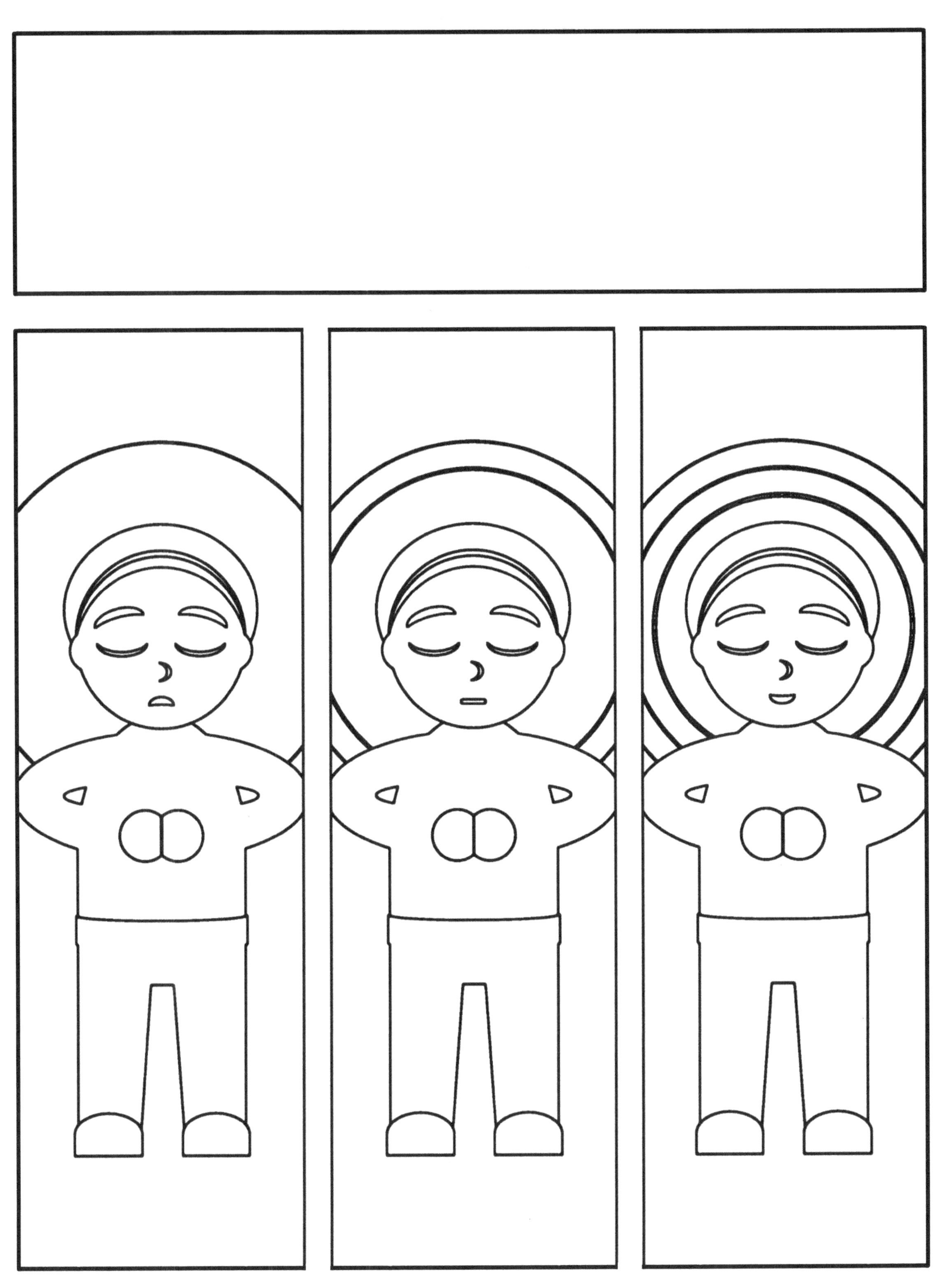

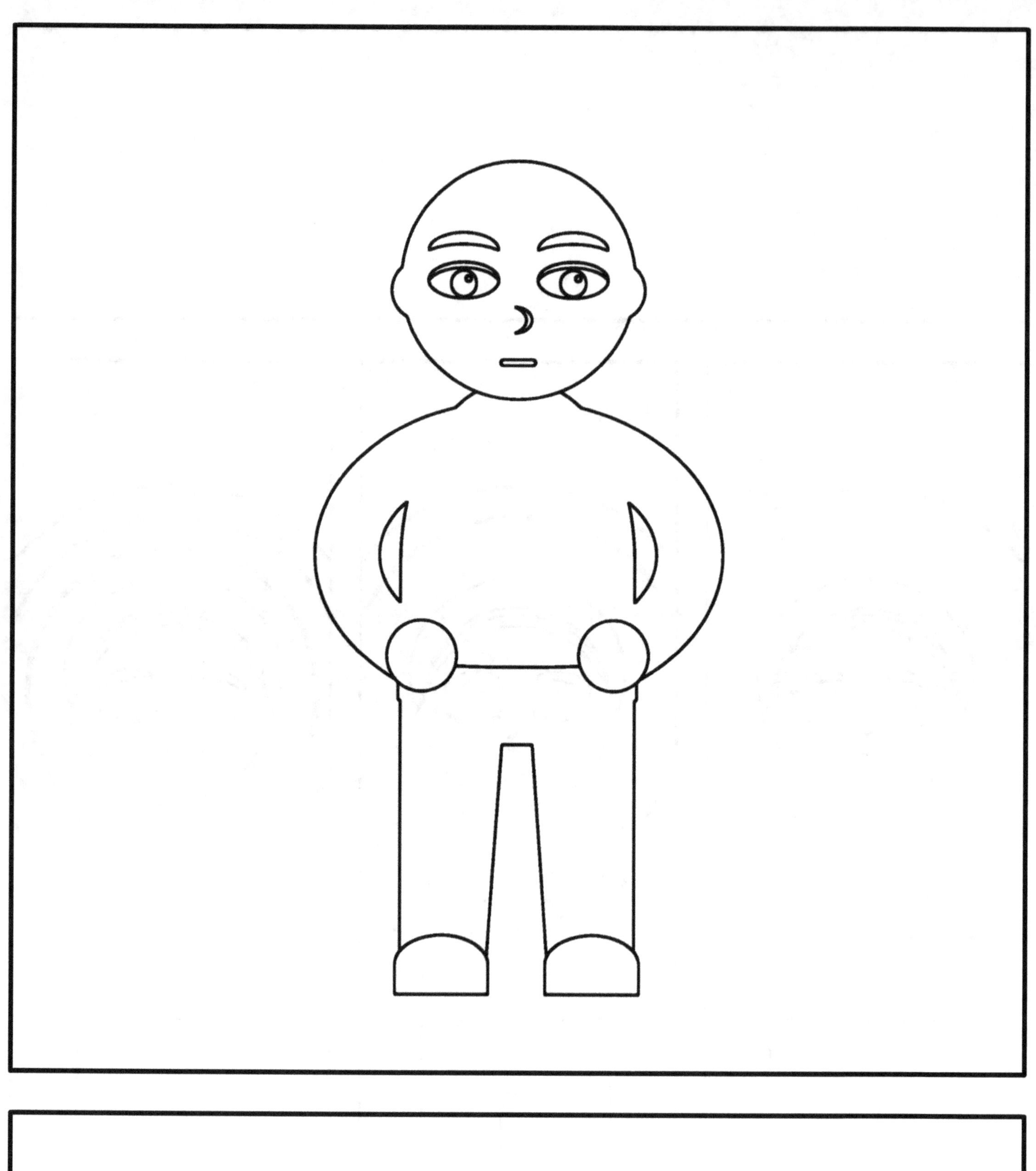

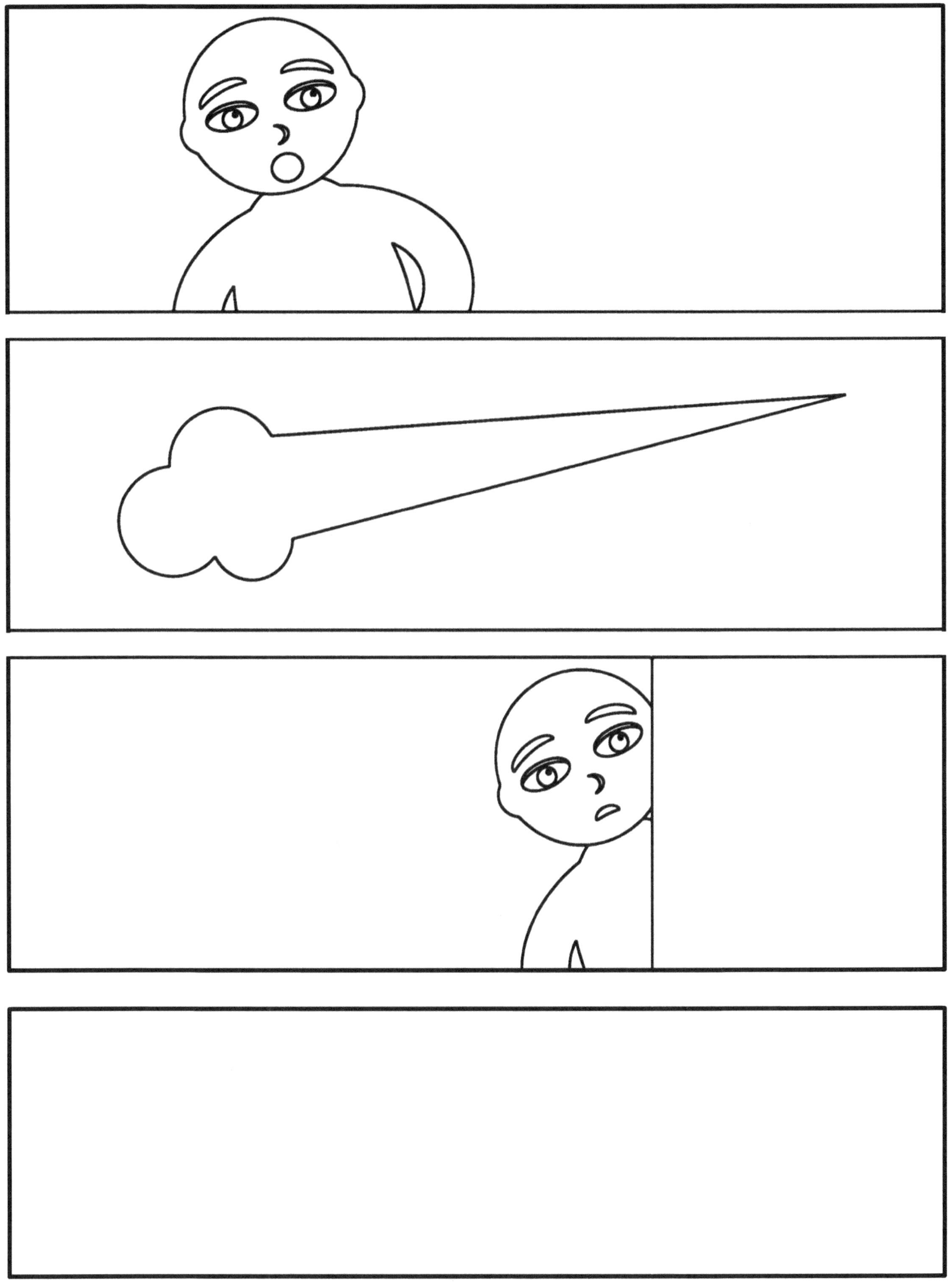

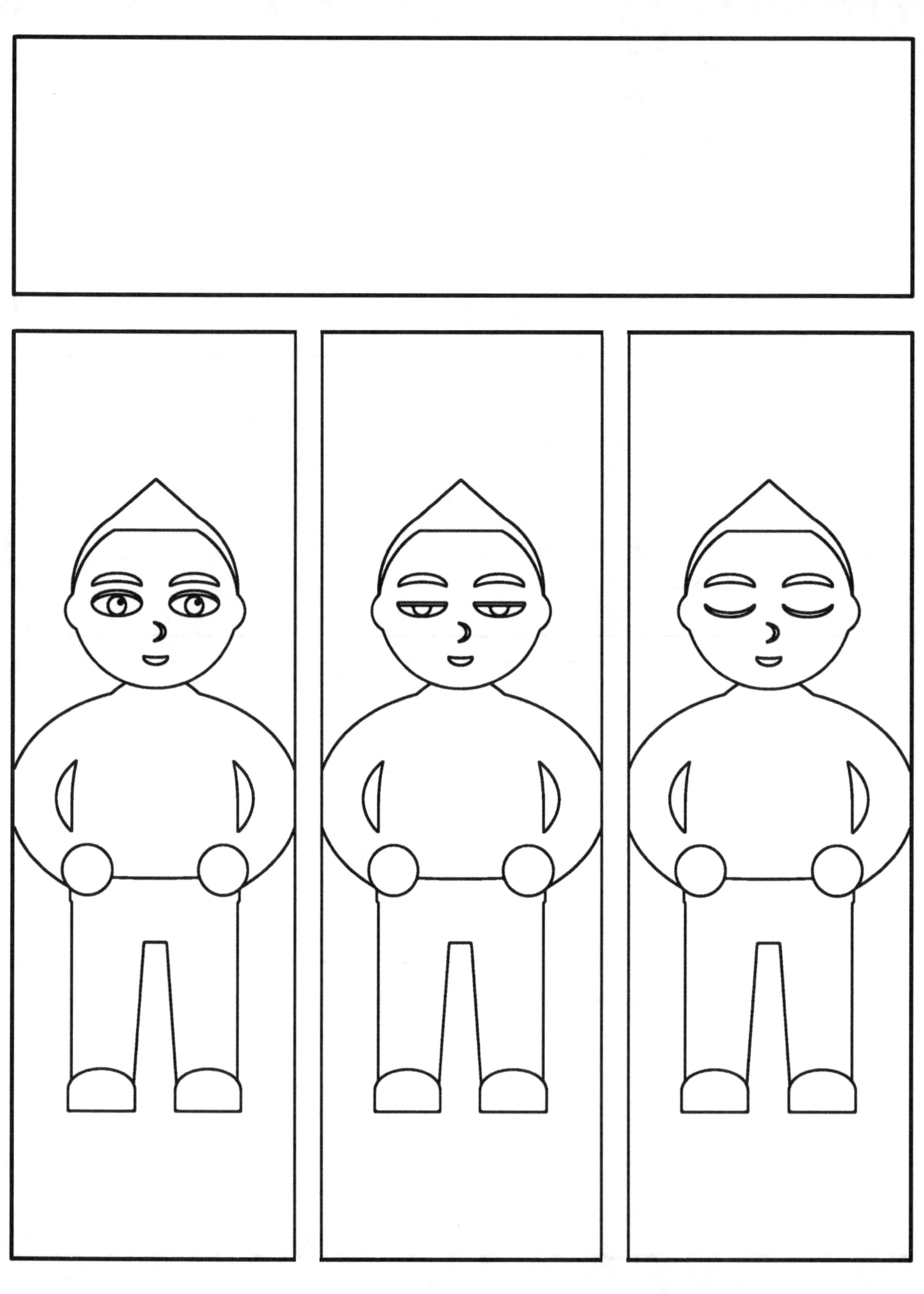

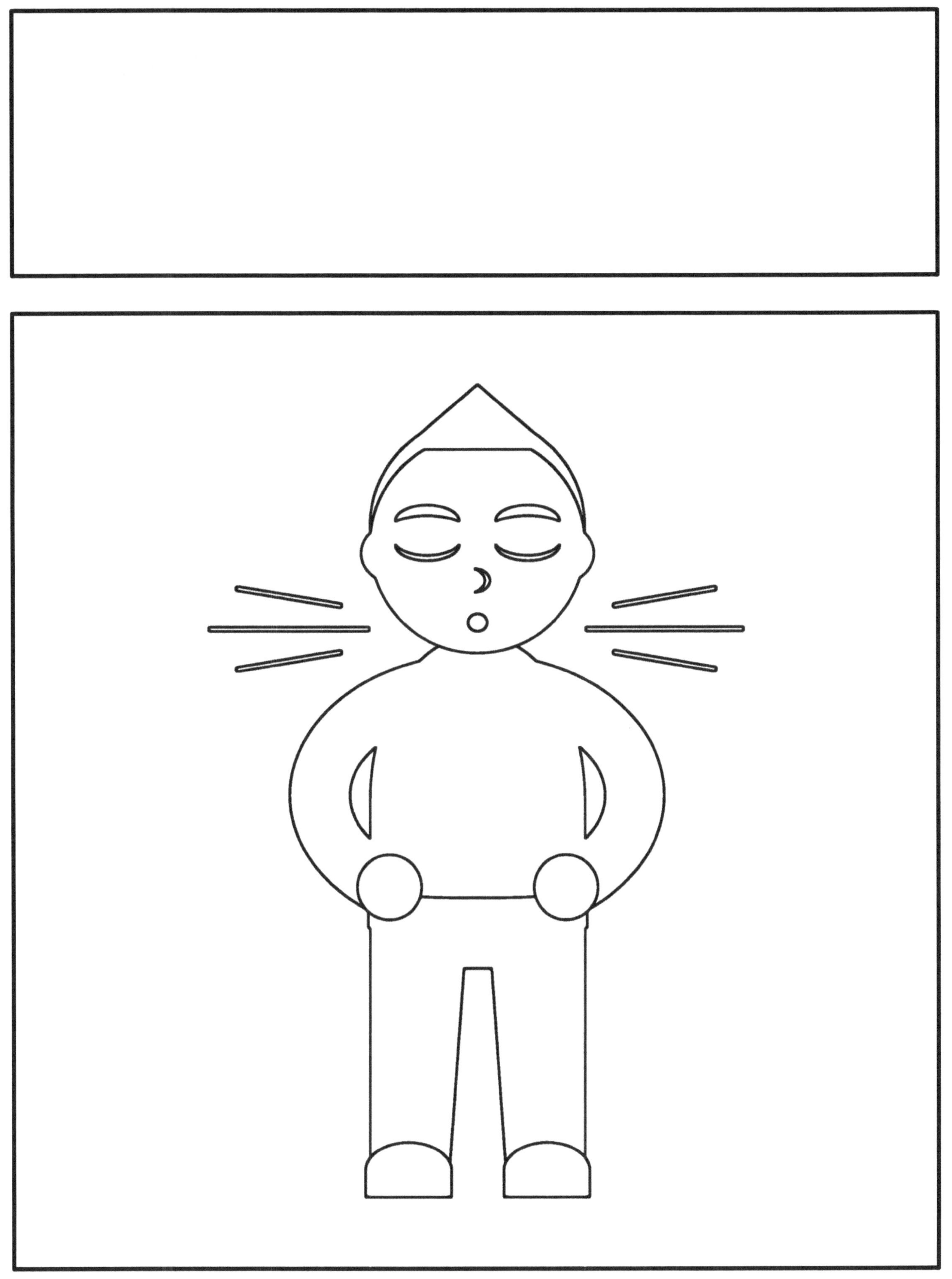

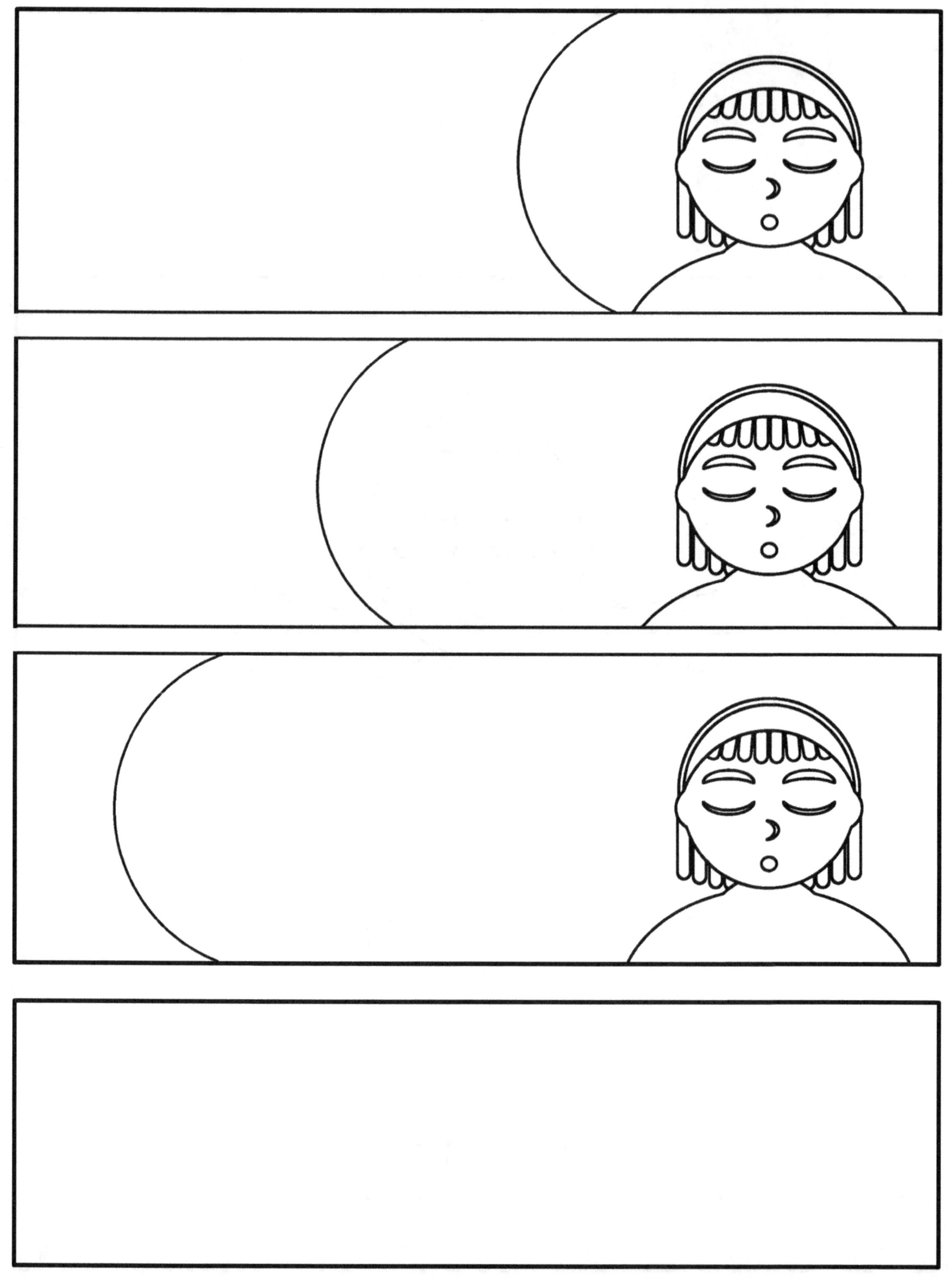

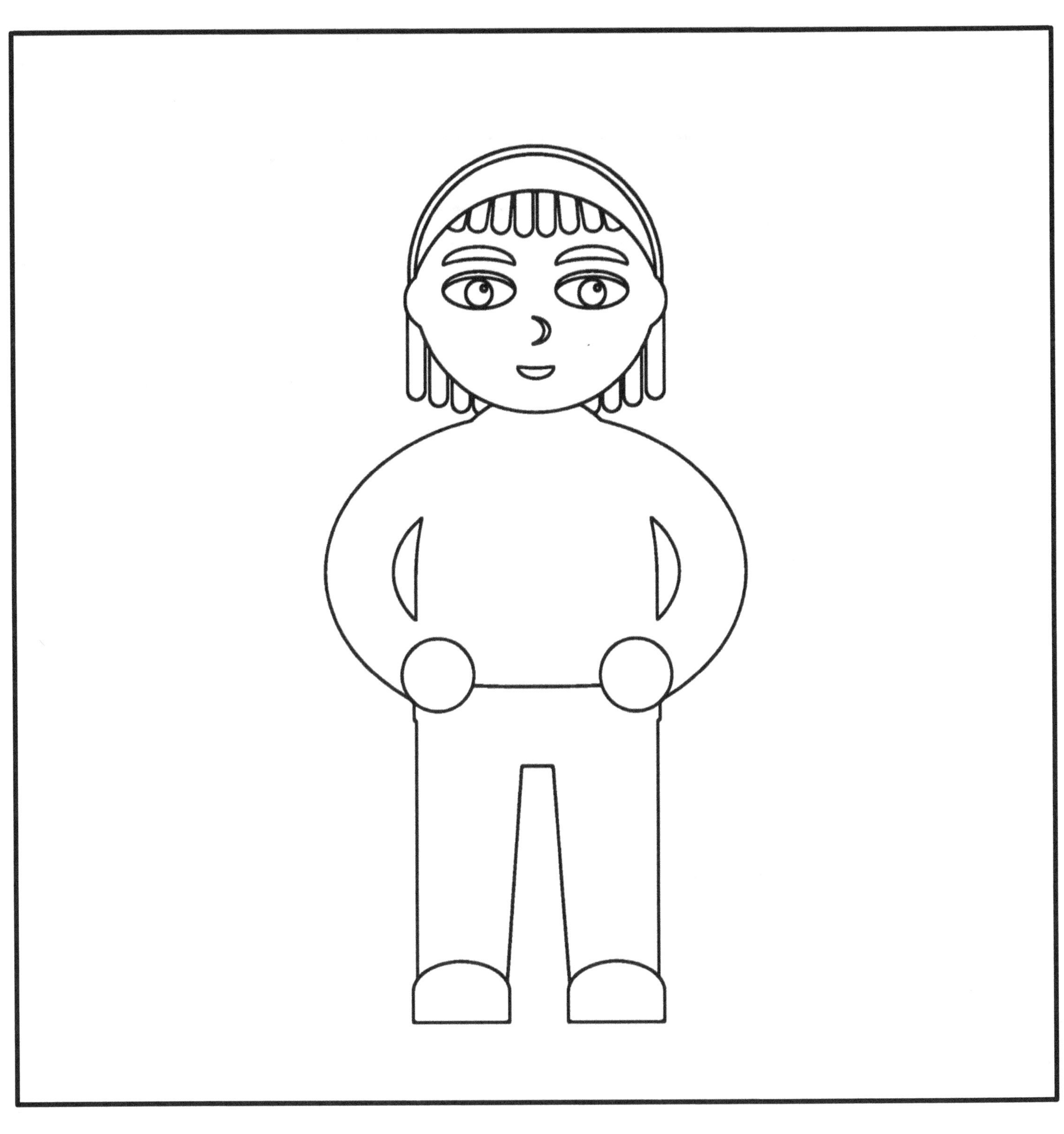

STOP
BREATHE

breathe
and
believe

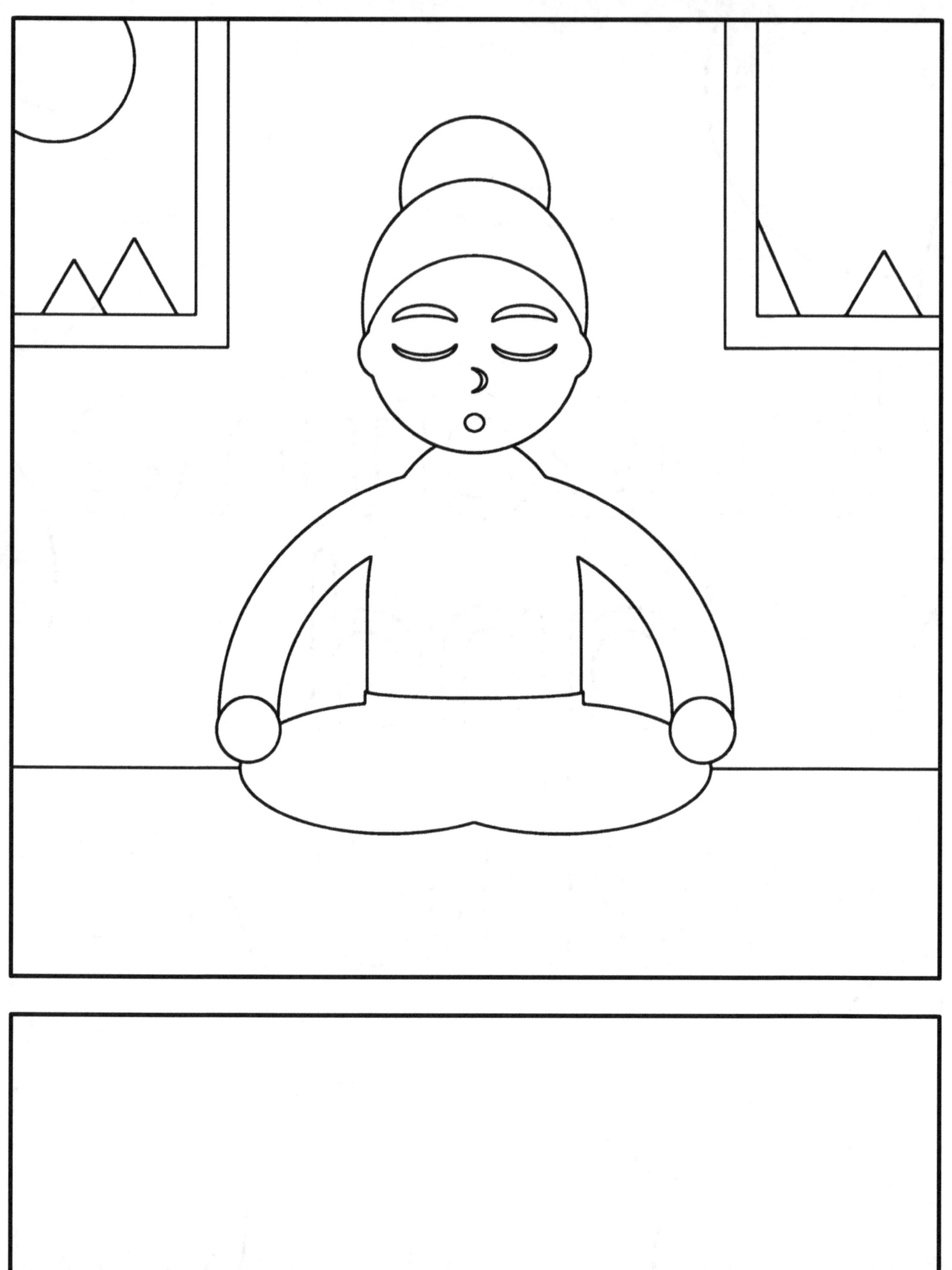

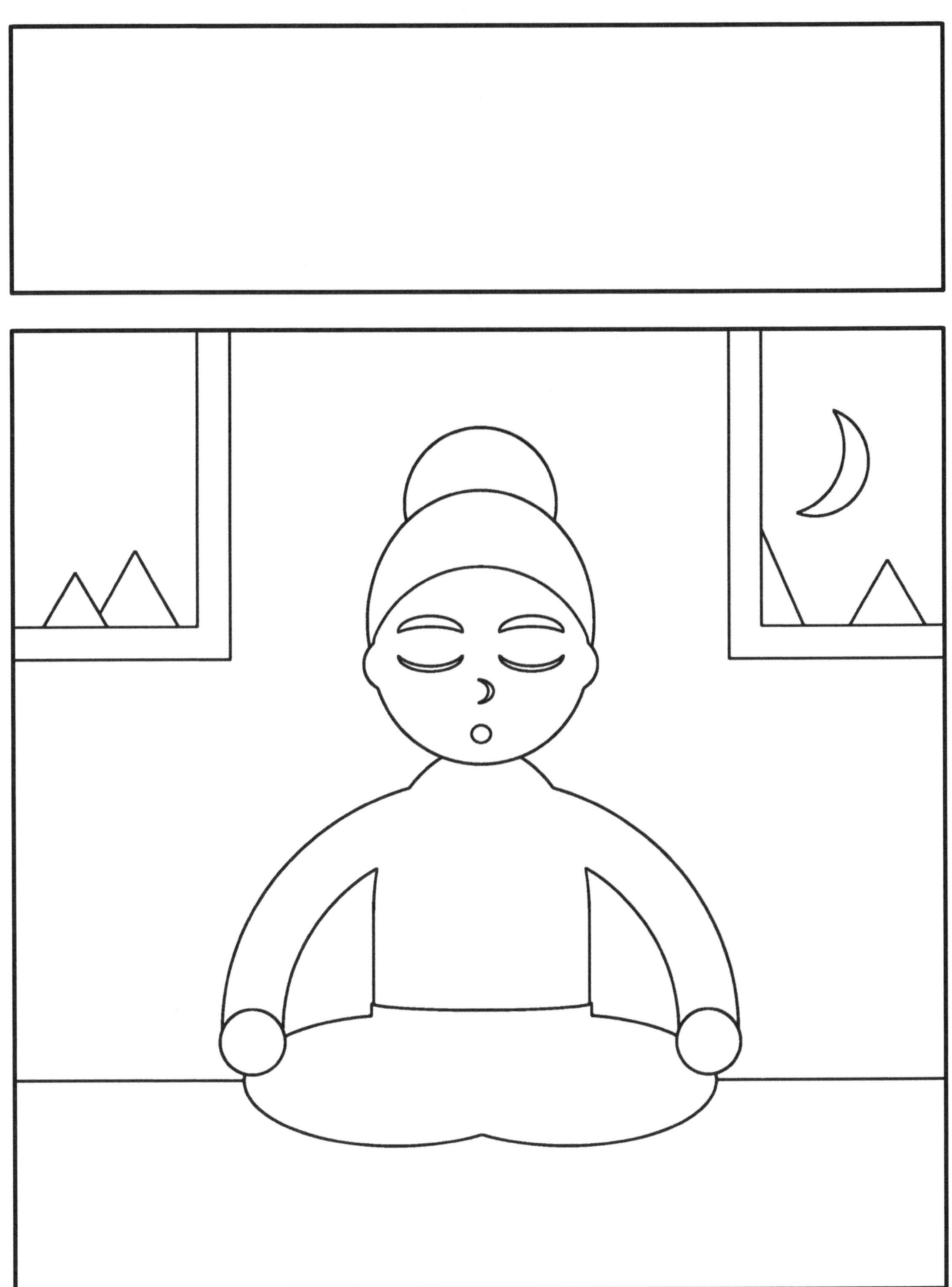

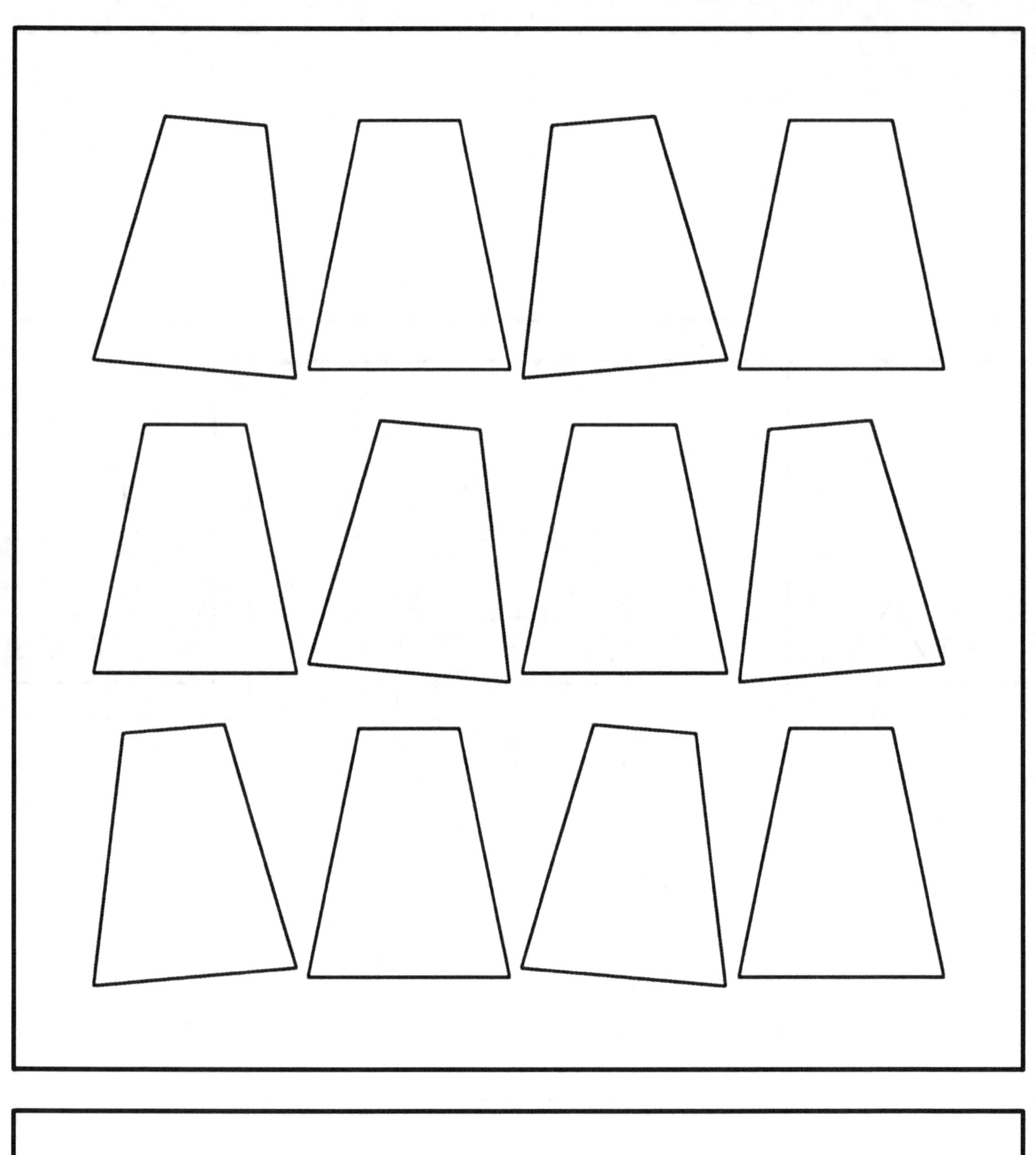

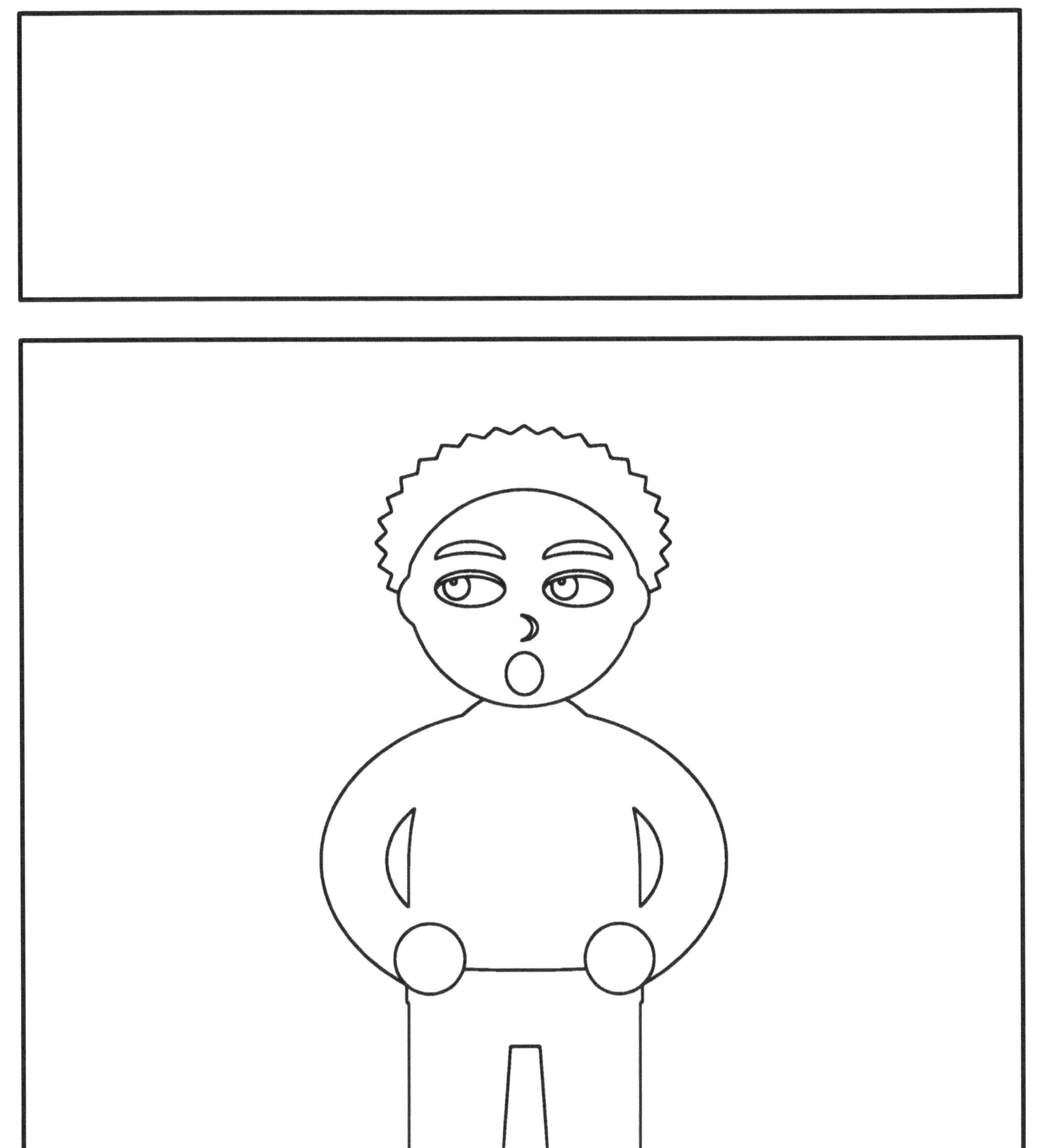

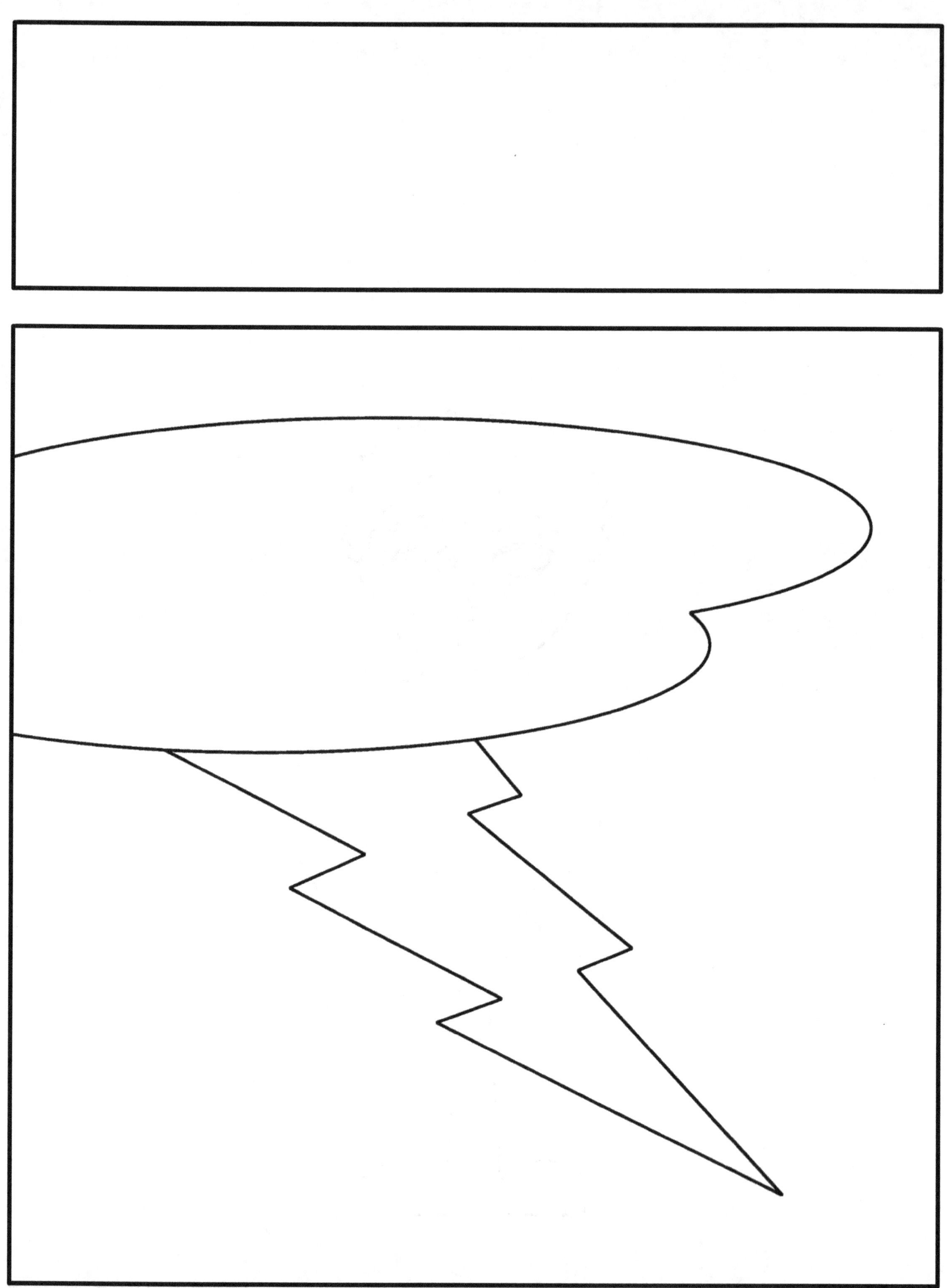

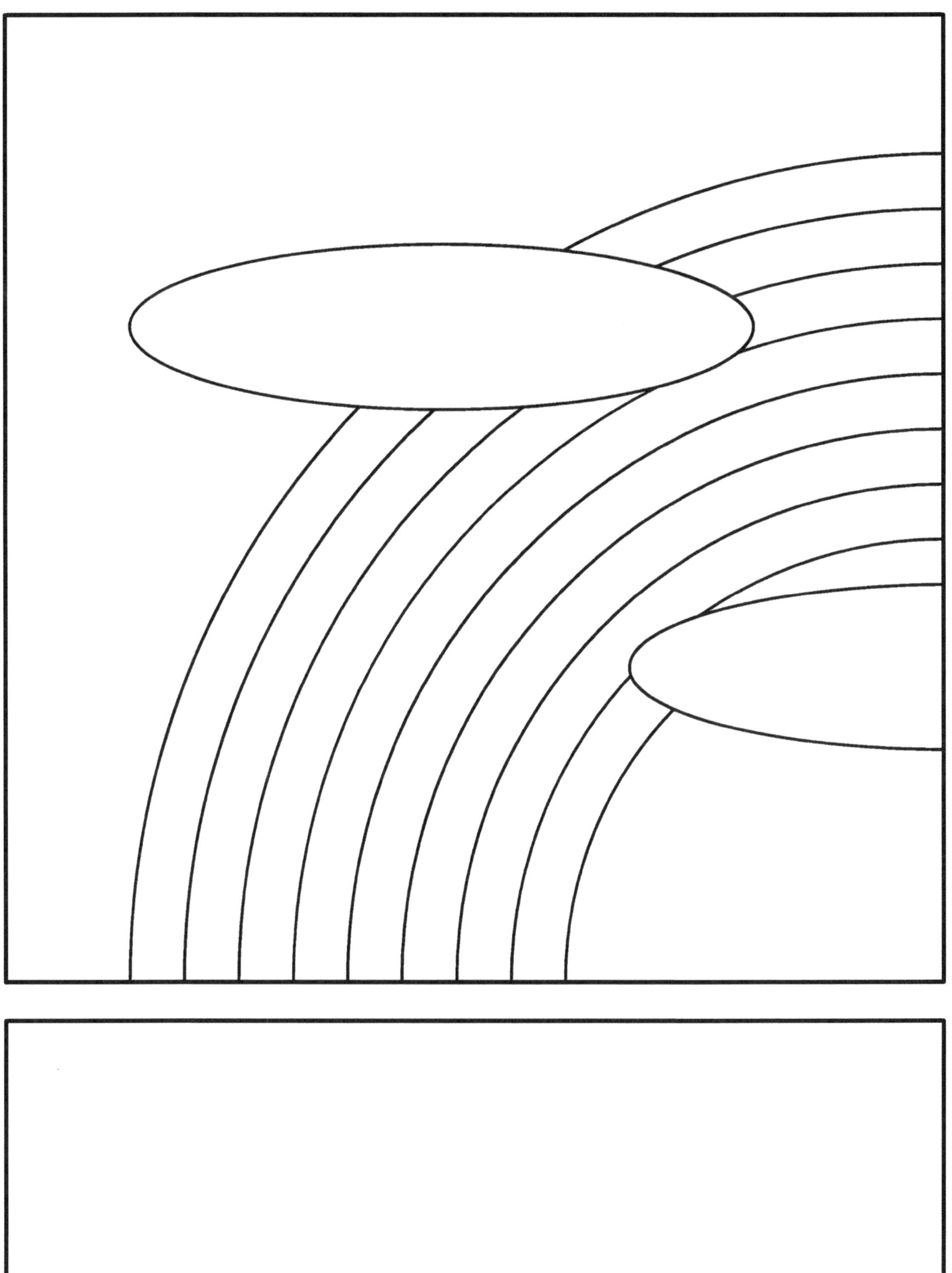

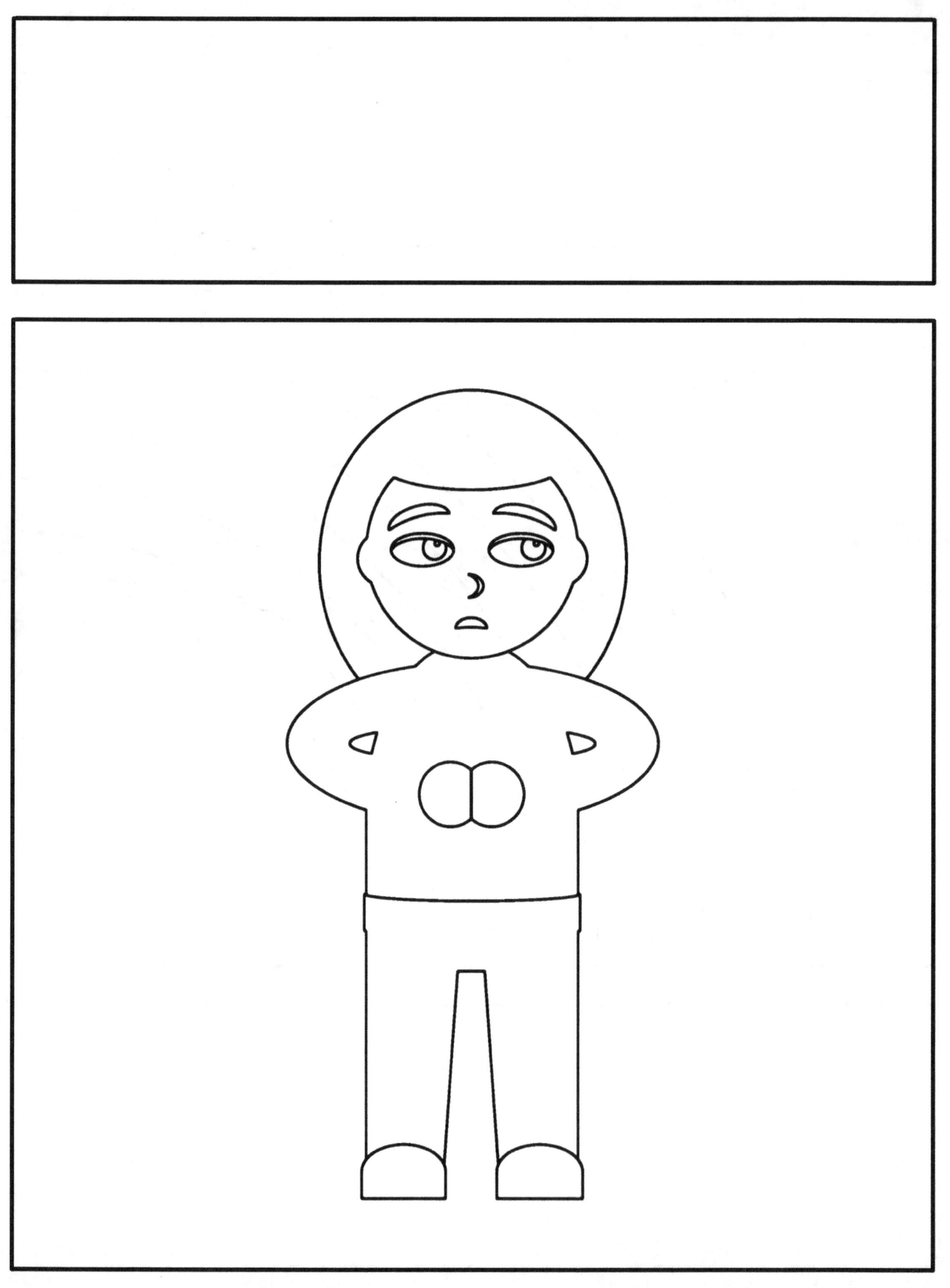

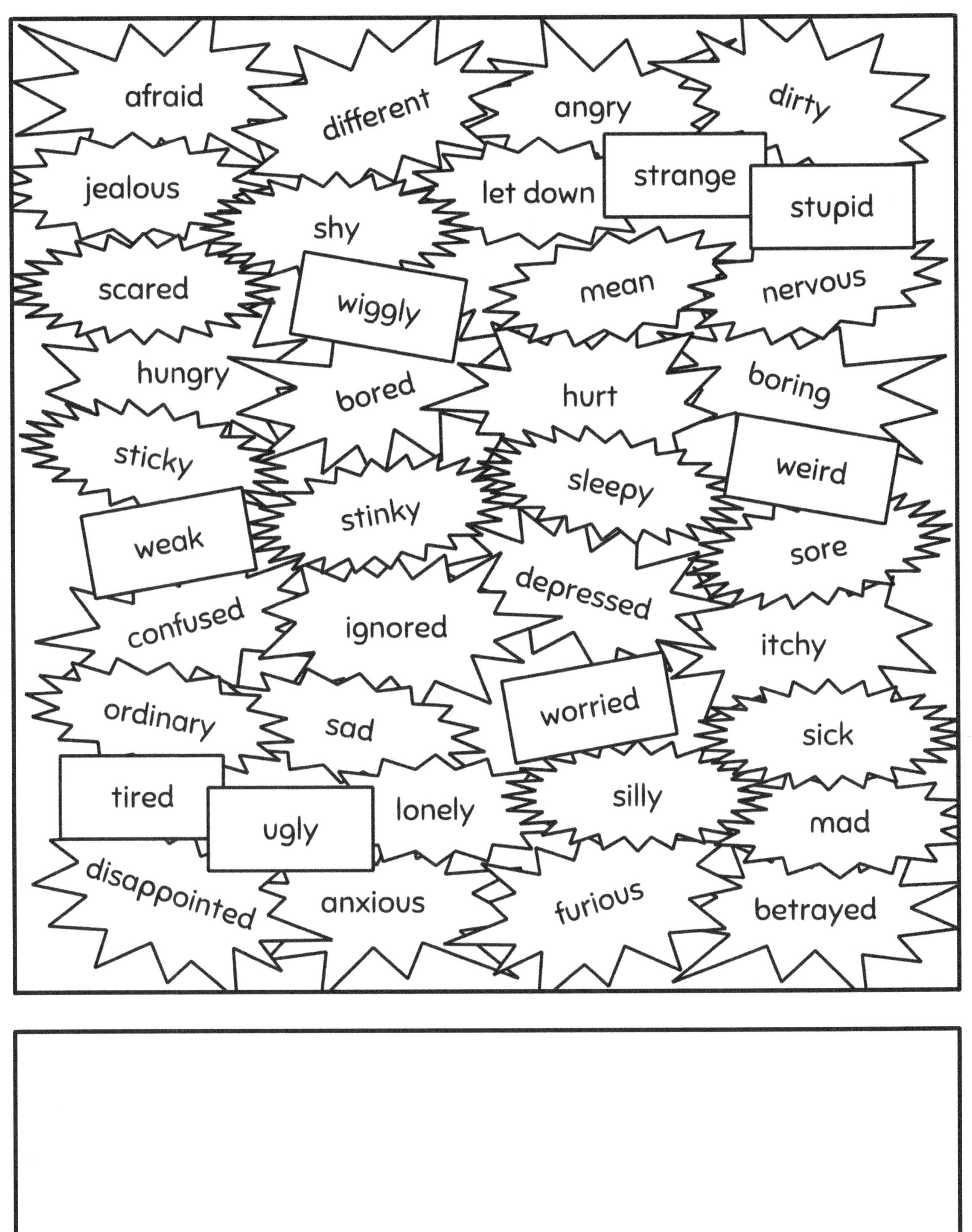

afraid
different
angry
dirty
jealous
let down
strange
stupid
shy
scared
wiggly
mean
nervous
hungry
bored
hurt
boring
sticky
sleepy
weird
weak
stinky
sore
confused
ignored
depressed
itchy
ordinary
sad
worried
sick
tired
ugly
lonely
silly
mad
disappointed
anxious
furious
betrayed

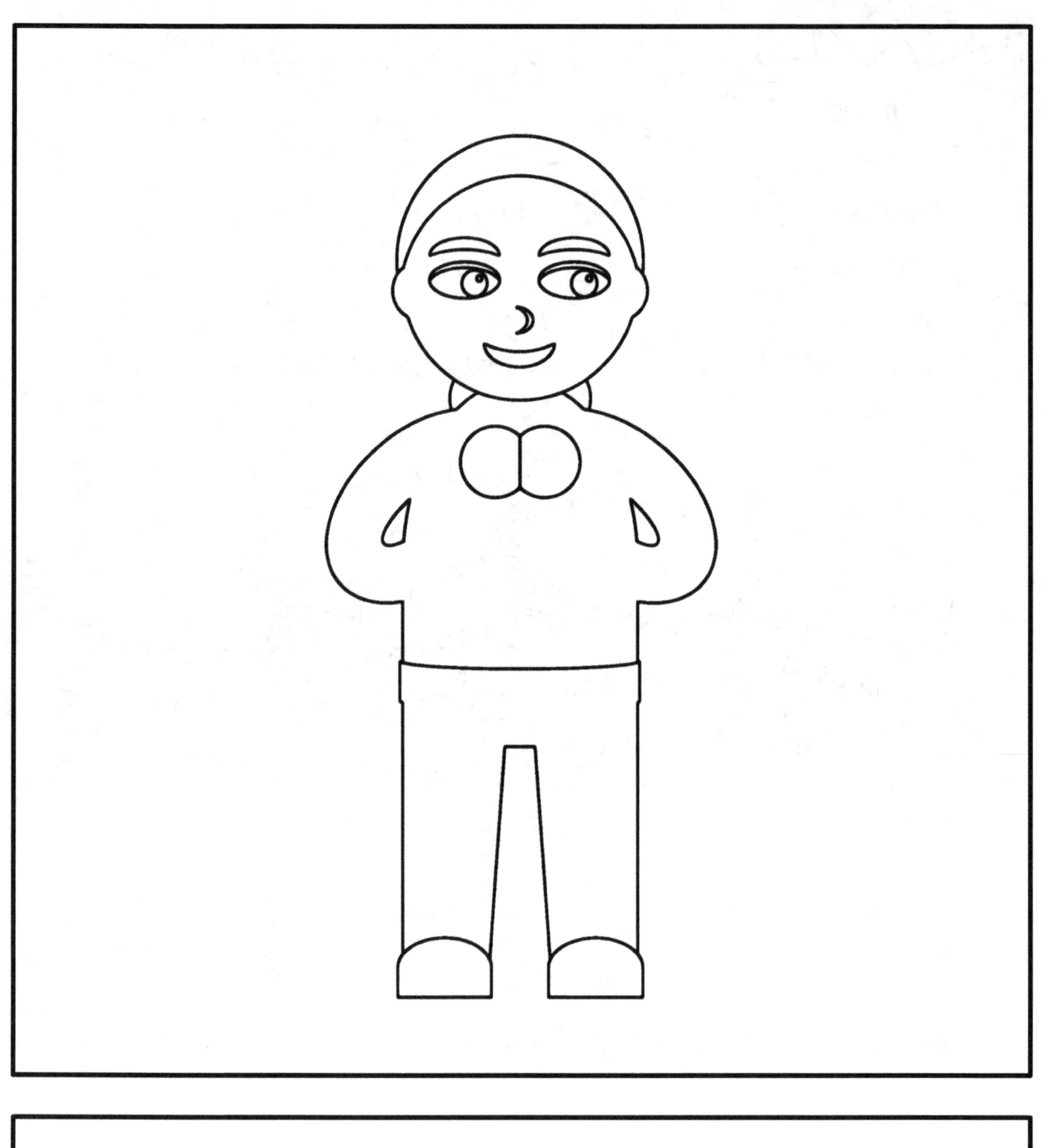

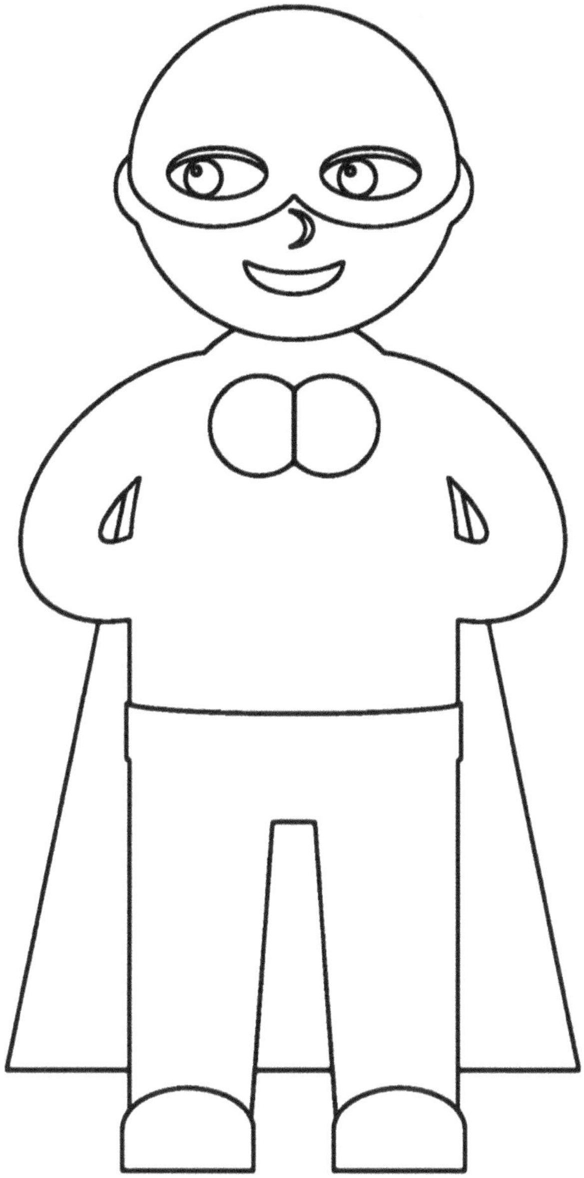

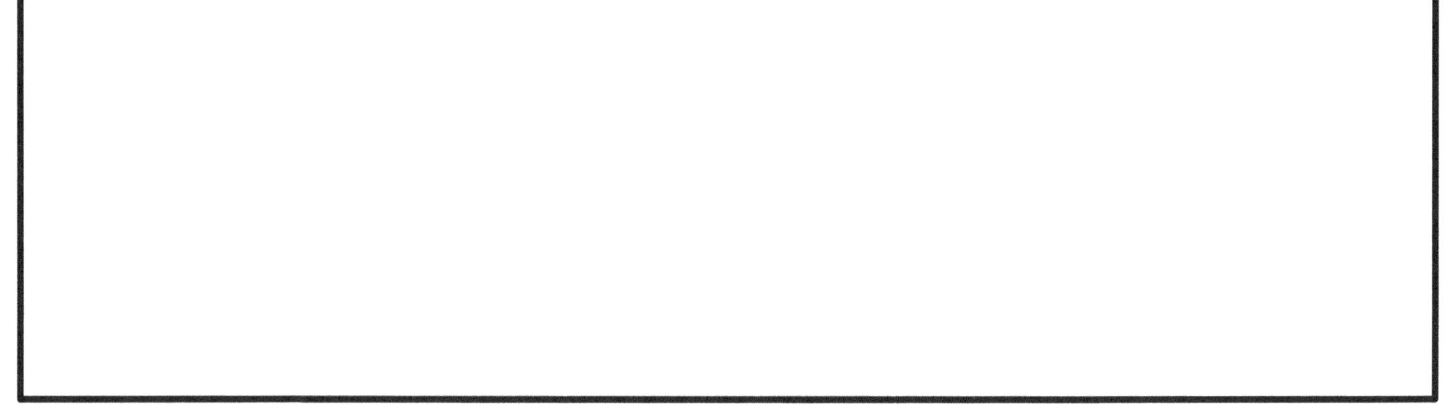

MY SUPERHERO CAPE

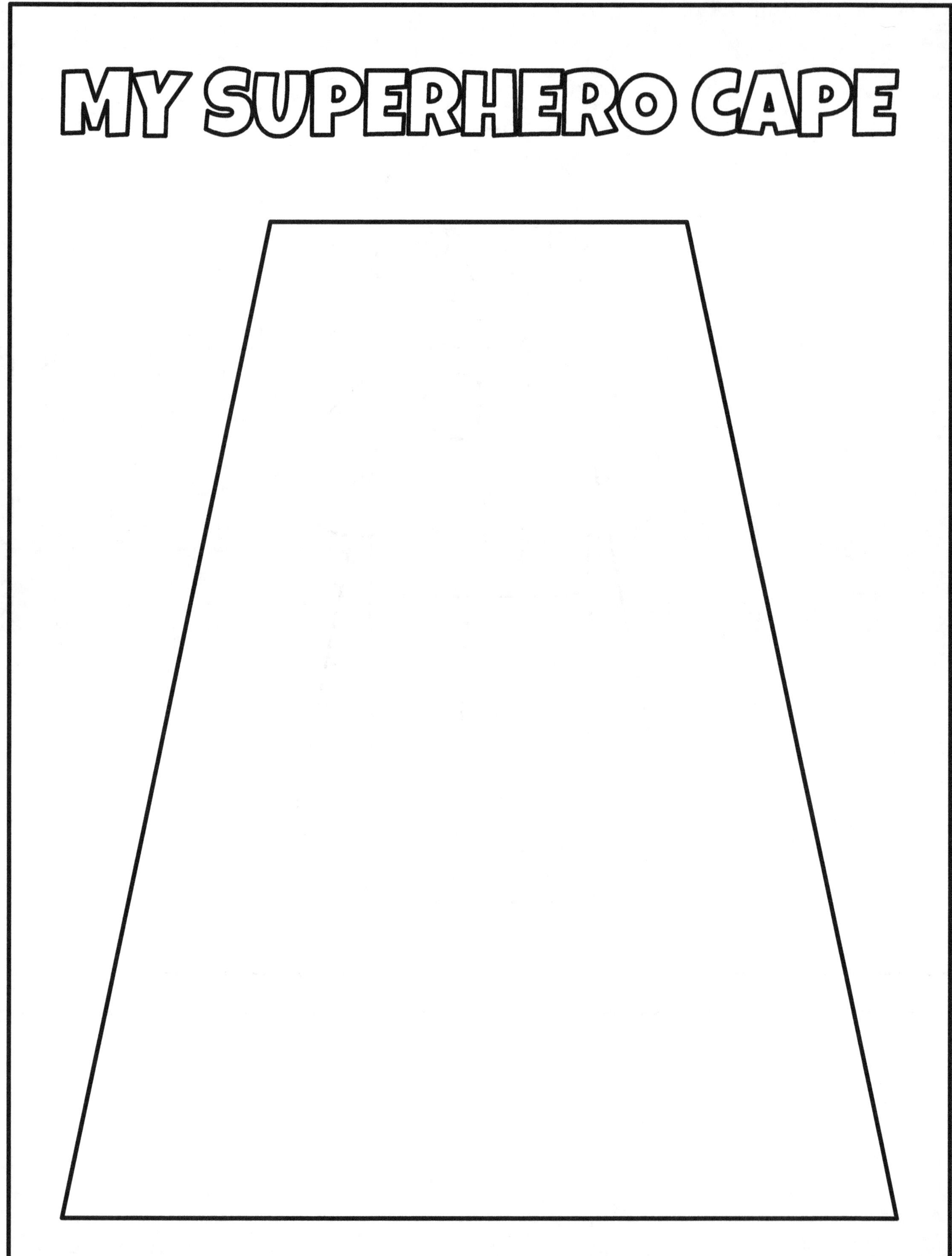

I have a
superhero
inside

MANY THANKS!

Dear Friend,

Thank you for choosing this coloring book! If you've enjoyed it, please don't forget to leave a review on Amazon, Goodreads, or wherever you're able to. Your positive review will help others find this book, too, and perhaps share it with others themselves. Even the shortest, most simple review makes a huge difference in helping spread the reach of this inclusive book, and more! Thank you so much for your support!